PRACTICAL
MINDFULNESS

PRACTICAL
MINDFULNESS

Simple techniques to become
calmer, happier and more
focused in daily life

KIM DAVIES

LORENZ BOOKS

contents

INTRODUCTION

Mindfulness is a strange and wonderful thing; both the latest craze and an ancient practice. Simple, but at the same time incredibly profound, mindfulness is an attitude of mind that takes time and practise to establish.

Being mindful means paying attention to the moment, which sounds like the easiest thing in the world to do. But it also means accepting one's experience, and this can be difficult. The marvellous truth about mindfulness is that you can start right now, wherever and whoever you are. You can dip in and out of mindfulness – and reap some of the many benefits it offers – or you can choose to make it your life's work.

How can one practice be all these contradictory things? It is possible because of the vastness of the central idea of mindfulness. Paying attention to the present moment, being aware of what is happening in the mind and the body, is by definition a multifaceted exercise. Our minds are as deep and fluid as the ocean;

The marvellous truth about mindfulness is that you can start right now, wherever you are and whoever you are.

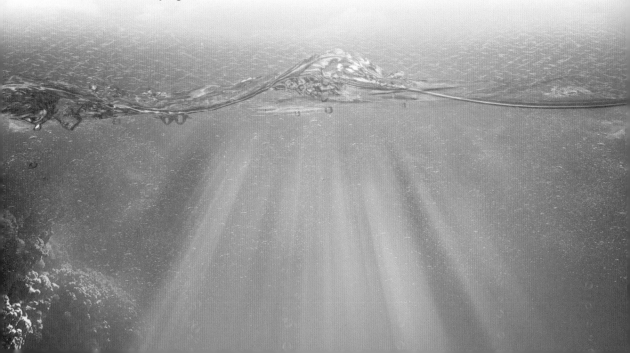

our bodies are an organic and ever-changing miracle of bioengineering. Most of the time we barely pay attention to our physical and mental being – and yet they are a mass of enormously complex processes. Focusing our attention on them, if only for a moment or two, brings instant and valuable benefits.

Consider how you ate your breakfast this morning. You were probably also thinking about your day, perhaps reading a paper, half-watching TV or listening to the radio, checking your emails on your phone, looking around the room and wishing it was tidier, thinking about the day ahead, worrying about some looming

Buddhist insights

This book, and many mindfulness practitioners in general, quote the Buddha from time to time. But in mindfulness, the words of Buddha are not scripture – like, say, verses of the Koran or the Bible. They are simply the useful insights of a teacher – albeit a very great and gifted one. The current interest in mindfulness partly stems from the fact that it can be approached in a completely non-religious way. Even so, acknowledging its spiritual roots helps us to understand the incredible power of the practice.

problem... So, although part of your attention was on your eating, much of it was elsewhere – you may not have really savoured what you were tasting, or been aware of how your body was feeling, or even what you were thinking about.

Mindfulness is about changing that half-conscious attention to full purposeful awareness. When we are mindful, we are fully aware of what we are experiencing – we notice what we are tasting, smelling, hearing, seeing and touching. And because we are paying attention to what is happening in the present moment, we become aware of the mind – we notice our thoughts as they appear, are present for a while, and then fade away like a walker retreating into mist.

WHAT IS *mindfulness?*

EMBRACING THE PRESENT

The truth is that most of us go through much of our day on autopilot, or else we are in thrall to the chatter of our own internal thoughts. This can often cause a disconnection with the present moment.

As we walk to work, we may be thinking of the events of the previous evening, an incident from childhood or perhaps an argument that we have had – these are all things from the past. Or else we are projecting into the future – worrying about what the day will hold, planning what we will do when we get to work, fantasising about winning the lottery. By the time we get to work, we may not be able to remember anything about the journey because we have not engaged in its reality.

Mindfulness calls on us to come out of future and past thinking – and to simply be in the present. The past is no longer here, the future has not happened. The only thing that is true is this present moment.

There are obviously lots of times when we need to think effectively about the past and the future, and not live purely in the now. Of course we often need to evaluate past events in order to understand them and our reactions effectively. And we need to project thoughts forward too, to plan

our time in order to use it effectively. We can still think about the past and future when we are being mindful – we can even enjoy a happy daydream. It is just that we are aware that we are thinking about the past and future. We are doing it on purpose rather than being swept back and forth by the blustery activity of the mind.

Mindfulness does not ask us never to think about the past or the future. It is not a form of hiding away or blinkering our vision. It is about noticing, and then stopping, the pointless unproductive musing that goes on in our minds – because this is what distracts us from the reality of the here and now.

BEING VERSUS DOING

In mindfulness we say that the mind has two modes, 'being' and 'doing'. When the brain is in 'doing' mode, it is focused outwards, on achievement and problem-solving. The 'doing' mind seeks to judge, categorise, create, compare. The doing mode is essential in everyday life. The 'doing' mode is what we use when we need to progress our work, meet deadlines, make a list, put up a shelf.

Our minds are brilliant at conceiving an idea and taking steps to accomplish it. The problem comes when we no longer need to achieve or solve problems. At this point, we should be able to shift into a more restful 'being' mode – but we all find

it very hard to flick that switch: our mind wants to keep on processing, even when what it are doing is pointless or even potentially damaging to our well-being.

Mindfulness seeks to move the mind from 'doing' to 'being' by consciously directing the attention to the inner world – to our breathing, and to our body sensations – and also to the outer world as we experience it through touch, sight, smell, taste and hearing. 'Being' is deeply soothing, but it is does not mean turning the brain off like a TV. In 'being' mode we are very much alive to our environment, we experience the incredible richness of the world around us as if for the very first time. We are able to perceive the reality of what is, rather than the dream or illusion of what we would like.

WHERE MINDFULNESS COMES FROM

Mindfulness has its roots in Buddhism and has been practised in the West for decades by Buddhist practitioners. In recent years it has become more mainstream and its benefits have been subject to scientific evaluation.

Much of the credit for popularising mindfulness in the West is due to an American physician named Jon Kabat-Zinn. He studied Buddhist meditation, and adapted its precepts in order to formulate a method for relieving stress and managing pain. He called his method the Mindfulness-Based Stress Reduction course. His work has been key to making these ancient teachings acceptable to the scientific and medical communities. MBSR is now offered by many hospitals and other health

Mindfulness is simply a type of training for the mind. You can practise it and benefit from it whatever your own beliefs may be.

organisations, and in recent years mindfulness generally has grown in popularity, and spread far beyond its roots. Kabat-Zinn's method has become what might be termed a 'lifestyle technique', and is discussed in schools, workplaces and public institutions.

Its Buddhist roots notwithstanding, mindfulness is not a religion, or even a religious practice. It is universal – it is no more bound to a specific belief system than practices such as fasting, charity, or meditation. Mindfulness is simply a type of training for the mind. You can practise it and benefit from it whatever your own beliefs may be.

Mindfulness is a serious and ongoing attempt to live each moment fully, and

build your self-awareness. When you are more aware, you become able to notice and neutralise a negative impulse before you act on it. This can act as a call to change, and can improve the conduct of your own life.

There are many misconceptions about what mindfulness is – and about whom it should be for. Here are a few other things that it is not.

• Mindfulness is not the same as meditation, and you do not need to sit on the floor in a particular pose to practise it. Meditation is certainly a positive element of mindfulness training, but mindfulness itself is an attitude that you learn to apply to the normal events, routines and activities in your day.

• Mindfulness is not difficult. In fact, you can't fail. All you can do is get better at it.

• Mindfulness is not just for certain types of people. Anyone can benefit from it. If you are the sort of person who can't bear to sit still, don't think you cannot meditate – you can. But you need to start small and train yourself to do it, little by little.

• Mindfulness doesn't mean changing your lifestyle. In time the awareness that comes with mindfulness may mean that you make different choices in life, but you can incorporate the principles of mindfulness into any lifestyle.

MINDFULNESS AND ME

When we say that mindfulness is a quick fix, we mean that it can take you to the pure essence of the moment, which can make stress melt away, but the real benefits of mindfulness emerge over time with sustained practise.

There have been many studies that attest to the benefits of mindfulness. Here are some positive changes you might see.

INCREASED SELF-AWARENESS

Mindfulness encourages us to look inward and pay attention to the experience of the body and mind, just as it is in the present moment. When we do this, many of the layers of story-telling, supposition and assumptions fall away. As a result, we get to know ourselves better.

BETTER CHOICES

When you are more aware and less reactive, you realise that you have a choice about the way you respond at any given moment. When our emotions and random thoughts no longer drive our actions, we are more able to assess the situation and make wiser decisions about what suits us. A study at the University of Mexico, for example, found that mindfulness training helped people control binge eating.

REDUCED STRESS AND DEPRESSION

Office workers who followed a course of mindfulness-based stress reduction (MBSR) reported a reduction in perceived stress. Another study found that people who suffered from depression were much less likely to have a recurrence after they followed a course of Mindfulness-Based Cognitive Therapy. The evidence is so compelling that this therapy is now recommended in the British health service as a treatment for depression.

IMPROVED ATTENTION SPAN AND MEMORY

Mindfulness improves your ability to pay attention, and also your sense of recall. In 2011, researchers working in Germany and the USA used brain scanning to show that participants who meditated daily experienced an increase in grey-matter density in the hippocampus, the brain area used for memory and learning.

STRONGER HEALTH

We know that depression and negative thinking can have an effect on our physical health. Mindfulness offers a way to reverse the trend: one study of people with cancer found that their immune systems were strengthened after following a course of

MBSR. A key way that mindfulness helps is that it makes us more aware of what is happening in the body so we notice stress and tension, and can take steps to relieve it before it becomes chronic.

GREATER COMPASSION

Mindfulness is thought to improve the way we relate to others. An experiment by researchers at the Northeastern University of Boston found that people who regularly practise mindfulness behaved in a more compassionate way so it may be that by cultivating a mindful attitude, you are also helping create a better atmosphere for those around you.

MORE HAPPINESS

Numerous scientific studies attest to the beneficial effect of mindfulness on wellbeing. People who practise mindfulness have been found to show greater activity in the prefrontal cortex, which is linked to positive emotions, whereas people with depression show less activity here.

START RIGHT NOW

There's no need to do any preparation for mindfulness. Here is a simple exercise that you can do right now. All you need to do is close your eyes and give your full attention to your breath.

In this exercise you simply focus on your breathing for one minute. It sounds very easy, but it takes all your attention.

1 Sit comfortably, either on the floor or on a straight-backed chair – sitting upright rather than leaning back helps you to feel alert. But if this is hard for you for any reason, you can do this exercise lying down or standing up.

2 Set an alarm to go off in one minute – or look at your watch and note the exact time.

3 Close your eyes and bring your attention to your breathing. You may notice the passage of air as it passes in and out of the nostrils, or be aware of the chest as it expands and contracts, or the rise and fall of the abdomen. Pick the place where you can be aware of the breath most easily and keep your focus there – don't chop and change.

4 Remember that you are not trying to control the breath by lengthening or deepening it. You are simply trying to notice it go into the body and out again. If it does deepen or lengthen naturally, that is fine, of course. But controlling your breath isn't the point of the exercise.

5 Soon – very soon – you may notice that your mind has wandered and you are thinking about something quite unrelated to the breath. That's okay. All you need to do is bring your attention back to the breath once more.

6 Your attention may wander several times over the course of one minute, and sometimes you may find that you have been lost in thought for quite some time. You may feel bored, irritated, frustrated, or restless – or perhaps pleased that you are doing so well. All of these reactions are

Remember there is no right or wrong way of doing this exercise; it is really about embracing your experience just as it is.

very common, and none of them mean that you can or can't do mindfulness. Just keep gently bringing your attention back to the breath, however many times you need to do so.

7 Remember there is no right or wrong way of doing this exercise; it is really about embracing your experience just as it is. When the alarm sounds, open your eyes and get up slowly.

attitudes

AND OBSTACLES

KEY ATTITUDES OF MINDFULNESS

Mindfulness is more than being aware. It encompasses a range of helpful and positive attitudes that can transform your approach to life. It's not just what you do, it's also about the manner in which you meet life's events.

It stands to reason that attitude of mind can have a profound impact on determining our experience. If you hate public speaking, then your nervousness may be apparent in your voice. That can lead to embarrassment – the very thing you were dreading. So if only you could defuse the initial attitude, you might be able to stand up and make a speech that is a true, unspoiled expression of yourself.

Or, to take another example, maybe you think that meditation sounds difficult. If so, you may put off sitting down to try it, or give up at the first obstacle saying 'I knew it was going to be hard. There was no point trying.' Alternatively perhaps you think it is going to be easy – after all, how difficult can observing your breath be? In this case when faced with an obstacle, you may feel discouraged or irritated. It is far better to approach this – or anything – with an open mind. If you don't know how it is going to be for you, why not just try it and find out?

Generally speaking, human beings like certainty and knowing. Mindfulness reminds us to be open to not knowing, to be comfortable with uncertainty. So attitude is

when we are truly in the moment, and we can also make a conscious effort to cultivate them, both separately and together.

1 Beginner's mind – the ability to look afresh at your experience.

2 Curiosity – approaching an experience with interest and investigation.

3 Non-judgement – sensing the raw data of an experience, without clouding it by labelling it as good or bad.

4 Acceptance – allowing your experience to be as it is, without trying to change it.

5 Patience – letting an experience unfold without trying to hasten it or delay it.

6 Trust – belief in yourself and the confidence that you are the best person to observe yourself.

7 Letting go – we have a tendency to hold on to thoughts and emotions, opinions and beliefs. In mindfulness, we allow them to arise, be present and then pass.

8 Non-striving – rather than rushing towards a goal, let things be as they are.

9 Compassion – being kind to others, but also to yourself.

key. The kind of openness that we are aiming for might not always come easily, but the more we practise mindfulness, the more naturally it comes. Listed here are the 'helpful attitudes' that we can bring to mindfulness practice. Each one is discussed more fully on the following pages. These helpful attitudes naturally come into play

Mindfulness reminds us to be open to not knowing, to be comfortable with uncertainty.

BEGINNER'S MIND

When we are mindful, we try to treat each moment as something new and fresh. The phrase 'beginner's mind' describes the attempt to greet our experience with the joyous engagement that a newcomer might have.

In mindfulness, we aim to view each event as if it were the very first time we had experienced it – which, if you think about it, is exactly the case. We may have drunk many cups of tea, but we have never before drunk this particular cup of tea, in this particular moment. We have taken many breaths and many steps, but never before have we taken this breath, this step

– and we will never again experience it. Children epitomise the beginner's mind because they are generally unburdened by preconceptions. Long experience has not left them with a 'seen-it-done-it' attitude.

If you give a very young child a colourful rattle to hold, he or she will look at it, touch it, shake it, turn it upside down. The child is fascinated by unfamiliarity, and naturally wants to explore it. In mindfulness, we aim to bring this same attitude to the present moment: whether we are doing something we know well or not at all, whether it is a positive or a negative thing, we explore it afresh. When you apply the beginner's mind, you are laying yourself open to an opportunity of discovery. In the words of Zen master Suzuki Roshi, 'in the beginner's mind there are many possibilities, but in the expert's mind there are few.'

The child is fascinated by unfamiliarity, and naturally wants to explore it.

Like Adam in Eden

At the turn of the 20th century a group of poets in Russia considered calling themselves the Adamists. Their aim was to experience the world like the Biblical Adam. They wanted to look at every object in the world with the same sense of wonder that Adam might have had on his first day in the Garden of Eden, and then turn that experience into verse. That poetical attitude is very like mindfulness, and is something that we can try to do – even if we do not then make poetry out of it. Try this exercise.

• Take a single flower, and then close your eyes for a moment. When you open them again, imagine that you are gazing at the flower for the first time, that you have never seen anything like it. What catches your attention first? Is it the colour, the curve of the stem, the intricacy of the petals?

• What else can you see? Is there movement? Is there a scent?

• Now try to look beyond your first impression. Perhaps the colours of the flower head are more subtle and varied than you thought. Perhaps the stem has a texture that you did not notice. Don't force yourself to see things; just let the nature of the flower reveal itself to you.

CURIOSITY

In mindfulness, we bring an attitude of friendly curiosity to whatever is happening. We cultivate an inquisitive frame of mind, and are open to being amazed – even by things that we have come to think of as ordinary.

The engine of discovery is curiosity, and it can be an immensely powerful impulse. Albert Einstein once said 'I have no special talents, I am only passionately curious.'

We tend to think of that kind of curiosity as an entirely active quality – as if knowledge was something that has to be dug up, like buried treasure. But curiosity – in mindfulness and in an attitude like Einstein's – is much more like a kind of attentive listening. It is a pricking-up of the ears, a level of high expectancy.

Curiosity in this sense is something we can cultivate in ourselves, and the outcome can be amazing. When we first hear about the practice of investigating breathing, it may seem like the dullest idea possible. But when we start to do it, we catch a glimpse of the layers of interest that are contained in a single breath.

Mindful curiosity is the urge to get a longer look, to watch as the layers peel away and reveal something deeper. It is the act of posing a gentle question – and

Mindful curiosity is the urge to get a longer look, to watch as the layers peel away and reveal something deeper.

being engaged enough to wait for the answer. Curiosity in general can be one of the things that drive our mindfulness practice. It allows us to rediscover the world about us, the one we thought that we knew.

Investigate the answers to these questions – or similar ones that you come up with yourself:

1 What happens if I meditate for three minutes a day for a week?

2 How does it feel to be mindful during a work meeting?

3 What does my anger feel like?

4 How does my body feel right now?

5 Can I feel spaces between my toes?

6 What do I sense when I place my hand flat on a table?

TRY THIS: The WOW technique is a fun way of exploring an everyday activity with curiosity. All it involves is applying the idea that each and every thing you experience is amazing and new – worthy of a WOW! Try taking a shower – WOW, this shampoo smells so fruity; WOW, droplets are forming on the tiles – how beautiful; WOW, I can really feel the heat of the water on my body – amazing…

NON-JUDGEMENT

In mindful practice, non-judgement is the knack of creating a little space between what is happening, and what we think or feel about it. We can use that pause to choose a right course of action if we need to.

Judgement is an essential part of the way that we learn about the world. It is a natural tendency of the mind to assess and evaluate everything that we experience. But the process of judging can become so swift that we do not notice that it is happening – and often it can blind us to the reality of the situation we are experiencing.

When we start to pay attention to our minds, we notice that they are ceaseless labelling machines. We classify and pigeonhole everything that we come into contact with: good or bad, necessary or unnecessary, mine or yours, and so on.

This isn't always bad – judgement is how we distinguish between the safe and the unsafe, for example, or draw back from something that is causing pain or burning without stopping to think about it. Yet

By divorcing experience from judgement, by peeling off those mental labels, we can experience more clearly the reality of the moment.

mindfulness asks us to step back and observe both the raw data of our experience and also the gloss that we put upon it. By divorcing experience from judgement, by peeling off those mental labels, we can experience more clearly the reality of the moment.

Imagine missing a train and having to wait. You may judge the situation to be bad – because you know that you hate waiting. But if you note the judgement and face the situation just as it is, you may find that you enjoy a few minutes of quiet, or that you take the opportunity to make a phone call you have been putting off. Non-judgement is about allowing ourselves to meet our experience with fresh perspective, about learning to avoid negative knee-jerk reactions.

One important thing to remember about non-judgement is that it is not possible to stop the mind from judging. So don't judge yourself for the judgements: that is a route to an absurd spiral of self-criticism. Just notice that the judgement is present and – as always – come back to the present moment.

Automatic judgements

TRY THIS: For half an hour, set yourself the task of noticing how many instant judgements that you make – this coffee is lukewarm, that woman shouldn't be wearing that top, this weather is awful. You may realise that your mind has a ready opinion on absolutely everything!

ACCEPTANCE

In mindfulness we pay attention to what is happening in the present moment without being distracted by internal storytelling. Acceptance allows us to be with whatever is happening without trying to change it.

We often meet our experience with a sense of resistance. Whatever is going on, we automatically wish to alter it or improve it. Even if all is good, we fret that this is temporary and worry about how to keep it going. This impulse to push away or hold on to experiences is so ingrained that we forget we have a choice – we can just experience the moment as it is. This is real, positive acceptance.

Acceptance is often misunderstood. People can see it as apathy or defeatism. But acceptance doesn't mean that we passively put up with everything that happens to us. If we are in an uncomfortable situation it may make perfect sense to take steps to change it. Say you are walking along the street without a coat or an umbrella and a sudden shower occurs. You don't have to endure getting wet. By all means avoid this by taking shelter in a doorway until the rain stops. Acceptance comes in when we cannot change our experience. So, as we shelter in the doorway, we accept that we are waiting for the rain to stop instead of worrying that we will be late for work, or agonising over the drops of rain on our new suede shoes. In the same way, if your routine is altered by a sudden snowstorm don't worry about what you can't control, enjoy it – make snow angels instead.

Those kinds of worries are pointless – we cannot control the weather, so our frustration is simply causing us unnecessary pain. Mindfulness teaches that we notice it is raining and adapt to it, we wait until it stops or perhaps we make the decision to go on our way in the knowledge that we will get wet. Acceptance allows us to make wise and positive choices that are not skewed by our resistance.

ONE OR TWO ARROWS?

The attitude of acceptance has been summed up in the phrase *Pain is certain, suffering is optional*. We cannot avoid pain – all of us have disappointments, illness, injury and loss to contend with. But we can make a choice about how we deal with our misfortune. A mindful approach is to accept the event and the painful feelings that it engenders. An unskilful approach is to resist the event – perhaps by bemoaning our bad luck, raging 'why

Acceptance is often misunderstood – people sometimes view it as apathy or defeatism – but acceptance doesn't mean that we passively put up with everything that happens to us.

me?', blaming others, denying that it is happening or perhaps seeking distractions through food, alcohol, drugs, TV or other mind-numbing activities.

The Buddha likened pain or misfortune to an arrow striking a man in the breast; responding with mental anguish, he said, is like a second arrow. We cannot avoid the first arrow but the pain of the second arrow is a choice. By facing the initial pain with acceptance, we find that it is not as overwhelming as we feared, and – like all things – it passes in its own time. Through acceptance, we can come to terms with the intermittent harshness of reality.

PATIENCE

When we start to practise mindfulness, we become aware of a sense of rushing that is present in much of what we do. Patience is allowing events to unfold in their own time – whether we like it or not.

Much of the time, our hurrying serves no purpose. You have seen people race to be first in the queue for a plane, or overtake on a motorway – you have probably done it yourself. But everyone on the plane will land at the same moment; and when you are in slow traffic overtaking the car in front just out of impatience is pointless. That kind of rushing is literally meaningless; it only creates stress. We may feel a sense of urgency about preparing dinner –

everyone's hungry – but that feeling turns the pleasurable activity of feeding those we love into something negative.

Speed is not always of the essence. If things take longer than we foresaw, it usually doesn't matter, or doesn't matter very much. The mindfulness of patience is often a question of not harbouring unhelpful expectations, because expectations are by definition hopes or fears about the future, and so keep us

Patience is the ability to meet life's setbacks and delays with equanimity, or even a wry amusement, rather than annoyance and anger.

from being in the present moment. You thought the drive would take an hour – in fact it is going to take an hour and a half. This means your arrival will be slightly later than you thought – so what?

Rudyard Kipling, in his famous poem 'If', exhorted us to, 'Meet with triumph and disaster, and treat those two imposters just the same'. That is good advice – and it applies to all our little disasters too. Patience is the ability to meet life's setbacks and delays with equanimity, or even a wry amusement, rather than annoyance and anger.

TRY THIS: Next time you are picking a queue at the supermarket checkout, don't waste time assessing which one is the shortest or fastest moving. Go straight to the nearest one, and then use the queuing time to stand and experience waiting. Check in with your body and how you are standing, and attend to your breath – in and out. If you have feelings of frustration or annoyance about the rapid progress of other queues, or the person at the front who is chatting instead of packing, note those and keep track of how they pass and dissipate of their own accord. Perhaps your queue takes a little longer this time but your experience is likely to be quite different.

TRUST

Another attitude that we bring to mindfulness is trust. A sense of trust in the process of mindfulness can help you to get you started and it can keep you going when you face struggles and difficulty.

The concept of trust, like faith, can sound a bit dubious – as if you are signing up for something that you do not really understand. That is not what is meant by trust in mindfulness, of which there are various aspects.

TRUST IN YOURSELF

We all have moments of self-doubt, and some of us are much less self-confident than others. In mindfulness, we build trust in ourselves and in our ability to know ourselves; we understand that we are the best (the only) person who can know what is happening in our minds and bodies at any given moment. The Buddha advised that rather than relying on the words of teachers (or writers) we should accept something as true only when we have come to know it through experience. So, trust in your experiences and in your capacity for understanding them.

You may get some kind of instant benefit, but you may not. You need to trust the theory of mindfulness in order to continue with your practice during times of difficulty.

TRUST IN THE PROCESS

Numerous scientific studies attest to the benefits of mindfulness, and it can be helpful to look at these as well as to do your own research. But in the end you have to consider whether the idea of mindfulness makes sense to you or not. If it does, then go ahead and try it. You may get some kind of instant benefit, but you may not. You need to trust the theory of mindfulness in order to continue with your practice during times of difficulty.

TRUST IN YOUR STRUGGLE

As you attend to your personal experience, you may become aware that the same irritants crop up again and again in your daily life – perhaps a recurrent worry always invades your mind when you try to sit and breathe, for example. Mindfulness can help us to notice negative patterns, and eventually to take action to change them. This can take time, and there may be moments of frustration or despair along the way. Trust that your struggles have something to teach you.

TRUST IN YOUR BODY

Mindfulness helps us to develop a greater awareness of what is happening physically in our body, and – in turn – a developing sense of trust in its abilities. This means that we are more likely to notice the messages that our body signals – when it is uncomfortable, for example, or when pain occurs – and take action to meet its needs. Noticing the body is thirsty, for example, or noticing a need to stretch and move can lead us to act in more health-giving ways and thus may reduce the likelihood of ailments.

Do it your way

Remember you don't need to find mindfulness easy in order to trust. Just know that you – like anyone – can do it. Mindfulness can be explored in your own way and your own time. If it suits you to meditate in your lunch-hour, then do that. If you are a parent and cannot find time for formal meditation, then try mindfully playing with your children. If you have an idea for a type of practice, go for it – trust yourself.

NON-STRIVING

Mindful practices are not a competition. You are not trying to attain mindfulness more effectively than anyone else, and there is no exam to work towards. Non-striving is the opposite of pushing for results.

When we are striving, we are careering towards a particular goal – endeavouring to complete whatever we are doing so that we can tick it off our to-do list and move on to the next thing. You may notice striving in the body as tension, an inability to relax or settle, or an impulse to move forward. Or you may perceive striving as something in the mind, as you exhort yourself to get on with it.

In daily life, our striving can become relentless. Often we have to suppress our feelings – of tiredness or overload – in order to continue pushing. This causes stress, and is ultimately counterproductive. Mindfulness allows us to meet this tendency with non-striving, non-pushing.

Non-striving allows us to rest in our sitting, to experience our sitting without exertion or detachment – simply to be, or be seated.

At the least, dropping into this attitude allows us to rest and heal.

We are used to believing that we must aim to do well at everything we try, that it is always worthwhile to make the effort, and the rewards of effort are success and achievement. Mindfulness does not stop you from accomplishing things in your life, of course. But it is a way of engaging with the world that does not require you to strain at the leash. If we are sitting in a garden, we do not need to force ourselves to sit – we are already sitting. Non-striving allows us to rest in our sitting, to experience our sitting without exertion or detachment – simply to be, or be seated.

NON-DOING

Consciously stopping to strive is so much more than a break from the daily grind, however. It is a receptiveness to the idea of non-doing which, when it occurs, can lend an ineffable softness and delicacy to the quality of our experience. So, for example, we do not strive to observe the breath as best we can; we simply observe the breath. When we are working, we do not strive through gritted teeth to work – we simply do the task in hand. Non-striving is letting go of the need for effort where it is not needed. In mindfulness, there is no goal and no end-result – there is only the state of being who you are in this moment.

TRY THIS: Sit in a chair for one minute. Just sit, just be.... This simple activity should be easy, but it isn't. That's because we are used to doing and striving. The 17th-century French philosopher Blaise Pascal summed it up when he wrote 'All of humanity's problems stem from man's inability to sit quietly in a room alone.'

LETTING GO

This principle is another aspect of coming to terms with our reality. Letting go means not trying to hold on to experiences or emotions – being mindful of the fact that it is in the nature of all things that they pass.

Letting go is the ability to allow things to pass – good ones as well as bad. Just as we let go of each breath in order to make room for the next one, so too we can let go of stale thoughts, feelings, sensations. This is not a question of ignoring them, or pretending they do not exist. Letting go means that we simply notice our feelings, acknowledge their presence and observe as they pass away of their own accord.

In meditation, pushing negative experiences away is called aversion, and

trying to hold on to positive ones is known as clinging or grasping. Both pushing and grasping are based on the false belief that we can control our experiences. We cannot – and trying to do the impossible just leads to pain. Our emotions come and go like the changeable weather. When a storm rages, the only sensible attitude is to wait for it to end; willing it to end is futile. Longing for the sun not to set on a perfect day is equally pointless, because that desire propels you out of enjoying the moment and into sadness.

It is worth noting that we can cherish negative feelings as well as pleasurable ones. A habit of sadness, say, can be a Byronic pose – something that we believe makes us tragically interesting to others. Or it can be the mindful tribute that we pay to our losses and disappointments, a symbolic bouquet laid daily at an imaginary gravestone. Here too we can learn to let go, and we will probably be happier for it.

Letting go means that we simply notice our feelings, acknowledge their presence and observe as they pass away of their own accord.

TRY THIS: When a baby first learns to grasp objects, he or she does not know how to let go. When he or she discovers that opening the hand causes the object to fall the reaction is wonder and delight – just ask any parent who has repeatedly had to pick up an object. Take a soft object in your hand, then open your hand to let it go, note that you need to make an effort to open the hand. We can bring this same conscious choice to let go of old patterns of thinking.

COMPASSION

An essential part of mindfulness practice, compassion is necessary as a way of balancing intellectual qualities such as curiosity, and allows us to bring softness and warmth to our practice.

By being compassionate, we develop a sense of interconnectedness with others and with the world around us.

Compassion is gentleness and kindness, both to oneself and to others. It includes kindness to animals and the environment, too. Here are three important elements to our compassion:

• When we are compassionate, we notice our failings and our struggles with benevolence and understanding.

• When we notice with compassion our pain and difficulties, we also notice the pain of others and realise that we share our experience. Our neighbours, our colleagues, our parents, our children – they all struggle like we do. By being compassionate, we develop a sense of interconnectedness with others and with the world around us.

• When we behave or act with compassion we have the courage to face the reality of our situation and feelings just as they are – without exaggerating them or minimising them.

Compassion goes side by side with non-judgement, and is an antidote to the self-criticism that so many of us engage in. Many people find compassion the most difficult of the helpful attitudes to accept. It's often felt that compassion towards oneself is weak or indulgent. But compassion is very different to self-pity – which involves casting oneself as a victim, and exaggerating one's feelings or their importance. Compassion is having the mettle to look at the reality of being human, with all the messiness that humanity entails, and fully accepting who we are.

When we are compassionate to ourselves we may find that long-buried distress comes to the surface. We may find a sense of grief that it has taken us so long to be kind to ourselves. In mindfulness, we start just where we are and let go of the past, but sometimes we may need the support of a skilful teacher or a therapist to help us do this.

A gentler world

Having a compassionate attitude expresses itself in many ways. You may start to notice the struggle or toil of small creatures around you – instead of heedlessly breaking through a spider's web, for example, you might instead notice that the spider is engaged in the struggle of existence, just like we all are, and have the presence of mind to move around it instead. You may even extend your compassion to the plants around you, taking the time to tend a neglected patch of garden perhaps.

HINDRANCES TO MINDFULNESS

Just as there are helpful attitudes that we bring to mindfulness, so too are there common obstacles that we are likely to face. But know that none of them is insuperable: you can move past the blockages that you encounter.

There are many ways that we can work with the obstacles and challenges we face. Being compassionate is important – for you do not want mindfulness to become a stick to beat yourself with. Trying to keep an open, flexible mind about the possibilities is also crucial. But the foundation of any practice is a certain commitment: you need to make a clear decision to try mindfulness and to persist.

HAVING DOUBTS

There will be times when we feel over-whelmed or sad or angry. Paradoxically, it may be that such interludes become more frequent, not less so, once we begin to become more aware of our internal landscape. It can be hard to maintain our belief in the practice at such times. We need to look to the mindful attitude of trust (see pages 32–3) to help us through. We can also make space for our doubt – that means sticking with the practice even if we are sceptical about its validity, or feel uncertain about its benefits. You can even use your doubts as a way of being with uncertainty – a useful skill in anyone's life.

FEELING WE SHOULD BE 'GOOD' AT IT

There is a reason we talk about mindfulness and meditation as a 'practice', because it is something we work at, a skill that is acquired. So thinking of ourselves as 'bad' at meditation or mindfulness is like thinking of a toddler as 'bad' at walking. It is better to use the word 'unpractised'.

Although some people see mindfulness as a talent, like becoming good at playing a musical instrument. It is perhaps better to see it as an apprenticeship. No first-timer would expect to be 'good' at plastering or sewing, so we too must let go of a desire to excel from the very beginning – this is where the beginner's state of mind comes in. Over time, we become more adept at our craft, but it always requires our attention. By the same token, we ought not see a particular mindfulness practice as 'bad' or a 'failure'. Mindfulness and meditation are like life: multi-faceted and mutable. No mindfulness practice is an entire climate – so no practice is objectively good or bad – any more than sunny days are objectively better than windy ones.

The foundation of any practice is a certain level of commitment: you need to not only make a clear decision to try mindfulness but also to maintain your practice and awareness.

EXPECTING MINDFULNESS TO 'WORK'

There are many benefits of mindfulness, and it is natural to expect it to yield results. Although mindfulness can indeed give us an instant way to be in the moment, we should not expect it to 'fix' us or to transform us into beautifully serene beings. We are still ourselves, but over time mindfulness can help give us an objectivity about our feelings and thoughts, a shift that helps us to become calmer, but in a very subtle way.

mindfulness

EVERY DAY

START THE DAY

Mindfulness can be applied to the simplest everyday aspects of our daily routine. We can even turn washing the dishes into a meditative process. Here is how to bring it into the first part of the day.

Those first few moments after waking can be precious and beautiful – a short period of awareness and repose before the start of the active day. So avoid reaching for your phone and checking the weather or news headlines (or your work emails) and try not to start mentally compiling a to-do list or worrying about what you have to face or achieve.

Instead, as soon you come out of sleep, try taking two mindful breaths. Breathe in, noticing that you are breathing in; and breathe out, noticing that you are breathing out. Mark any impulse to rush this process, but keep your attention on the breath. Be aware of any thoughts as they arise, 'I can hear the children', for

Be aware of any distracting or negative thoughts as they arise – 'I have so much to do today …' – and simply bring your attention back to the breath.

example, or 'I hate my job' – and simply bring your attention back to the breath.

Try gently bringing your mouth into a smile – you don't have to force a wide grin, but the physical act of smiling has a positive effect on your mood, even if you are faking it. Take another breath – in and out. Open your eyes and get up slowly.

Aim to maintain this mindful awareness as you go about your morning routine. It is helpful to practise formal meditation first thing in the morning if you can, but if this doesn't suit you, pick at least one activity that you do every day and do it with mindful awareness. You can:

• take a shower mindfully
• brush your teeth mindfully
• make your bed mindfully
• eat your breakfast mindfully
• wash up your breakfast things mindfully
• drink a cup of tea mindfully
• focus on a beautiful object mindfully
• do a minute's sitting practice just before you leave the house

TRY THIS: MINDFUL BRUSHING

We know we should spend two minutes brushing our teeth at least twice a day, but plenty of us skimp on that. And while we clean, we often zone out or escape into plans or worries for the day ahead. Today, when you clean your teeth, use this time as an opportunity to engage the senses and be in the moment.

1 Take a deep breath before you start. Notice the intention to pick up your toothbrush – and how you distinguish it from any others in the bathroom.

2 Notice the feel of the toothpaste and toothbrush in your hands, and the actions involved as you squeeze the toothpaste onto the brush. Be aware of the physical engagement that you bring to turning on the tap and moving the brush to the stream of water, and then note the act of turning off the tap.

3 Notice the look and colour of the toothpaste on your brush, and how it lies on the bristles.

4 Bring the toothbrush to your mouth, being aware of how the whole arm and hand is involved in the movement.

5 Notice the aroma of the toothpaste. Mark how your mouth opens to receive the toothbrush.

6 Slowly start to brush your teeth. Is there a sense of coldness when the brush first makes contact with the teeth? What can you taste – is it minty or sweet? And does the toothpaste feel soft or gritty or foamy?

7 As you brush different parts of your mouth, what does it feel like as the brush glides over each tooth?

8 Watch yourself in the mirror as you brush. Notice any sensations that you feel in the arm and hand as they guide the brush around your mouth, and the feeling of the brush against the teeth. Hear the sound of the brushing.

9 Try to be aware of the intention to spit before you do so – what does that feel like? Keep your attention on your teeth as you continue to brush, being aware of any thoughts that come up.

10 When you finish, notice how the inside of the mouth and teeth feel, and the fresh taste in your mouth.

Seven ideas for mindful mornings
Practising mindfulness first thing in the morning is helpful because it gets you in a more aware frame of mind straight away. It's a wonderful time for a formal meditation, but there are many other ways that you can incorporate mindfulness into the morning.

• **Get organised** the night before – get your clothes ready, and prepare your bag with whatever you need for the day.

• **Get a proper alarm clock** – if you use your mobile phone as your alarm, then you are putting temptation in your way – it is too easy to stretch out your hand and check your emails late at night or first thing in the morning, both of which propel you into work mode when you should be at rest.

• **Notice your stressors** – think about your mornings and what causes you stress? If you often find yourself hunting for your keys, make a point of finding them the night before. If everyone wants to use the bathroom at the same time, think about changing your routine.

• **Give yourself time** – get up 15 minutes earlier than you need to. Use this time to do a short meditation practice, or to do something that gives you pleasure in a mindful way – perhaps drink a cup of tea in bed with peace and a sense of joy.

• **Greet the world** – open your curtains or blinds, and take a moment to notice the sky outside.

• **Prioritise** – lengthy to-do lists can be overwhelming. Pick the top three things you need to do today, and concentrate on those – one at a time. It can help to write your to-do list the night before.

• **Get enough sleep** – if you are feeling tired, it's harder to be alert and aware. Look at your evening routine to be sure you are getting the rest you need.

MINDFULNESS OF TRAVEL

Most of us do short journeys every day. Whether we drive, cycle, walk or take public transport, it often becomes something that is done on autopilot. That is a shame, as these trips are opportunities to be alive to the moment.

Not many people enjoy commuting. Research suggests that our feelings of wellbeing decrease with every minute that we spend getting to work. Often these daily journeys are seen as an ordeal, and there are plenty of reasons to dislike it – crowded buses, late trains, traffic jams, wind and rain, or simply the feeling that we are between places, inhabiting dead time. Our reaction to these things is often aversion – a pushing away of the experience. But if we cannot change our experience then, pushing it away simply causes us stress. Bringing acceptance to our experience can lift the difficulty.

Here are some tips on mindful travelling. As you prepare for a journey, leave yourself enough time to get ready without rushing. Just before you leave the house, sit for a few moments and pay attention to your breathing. Interestingly, Russians always take a moment to pause in their street clothes before setting out on a journey – a tradition called 'sitting for the road'.

If you are rushing, it is difficult to be aware, so even before you start your journey, slow things down. Just before you leave the house, take a seat for a few moments and pay attention to your breathing.

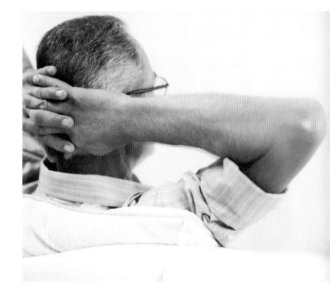

PUBLIC TRANSPORT

The most difficult aspects of public transport are the delays that might occur and the inevitable close proximity of other people. Reading or listening to music can be a pleasurable way of transporting yourself and creating a barrier, but this is an escape. Instead, use this time more positively to practise meditation or mindfulness. Try this technique:

• Focus on the breath between bus stops or train stations.

• Bring your attention to the sensations of the body. Can you feel the seat, the hardness of the floor beneath your feet? Let go of judgements like 'uncomfortable' or 'comfortable', and notice the quality of what you feel. Let things be as they are.

• Be mindful of sounds – the rhythm of the train as it progresses, the rise and fall of the engine of the bus, your own breathing, people talking nearby.

• Try the 54321 technique: notice 5 things you can see, hear and feel, then 4 things, then 3 things, then 2 things, then 1 thing. Use your fingers to keep count – you can use the same things each time or different, whatever comes to your attention.

• As you notice people around you, try to be aware of them as human beings who feel and think just as you do. Are you able to (silently) wish them well?

Whichever technique you try, you are bound to become distracted. Just gently bring your attention back to what you are doing. This can help you arrive at your destination more relaxed and refreshed than if you had been sitting there stewing at the unpleasantness of it all.

WALKING

When we set out somewhere, our thoughts often go to what we will do when we arrive – and before we know it we are lost in a random train of thought. Try to attend to the reality of each moment of your walk, without thinking about your destination. You can use the sensation of the soles of your feet on the ground as a way to focus yourself. Try it – it is more absorbing than you might think.

Notice as:
* the heel strikes the ground
* the rest of the foot rolls down
* you push off with your toes and ball of your foot

There's no need to walk more slowly than you usually do, just proceed at your natural pace. You may find that you start to slow down as you walk in this mindful way, this is fine, but don't actively try to change. As you walk, your mind will inevitably become distracted by what you see, hear, smell. Just be aware of what you are noticing for as long as it holds your attention – you may find something beautiful or interesting – then bring your focus back to your feet as soon as your mind starts to wander or the object of your attention falls behind you.

DRIVING

Driving can be stressful because it requires both focused concentration and a broad awareness. And yet much of the way we drive is automatic. We are barely aware of checking the mirror or turning the wheel – we do it instinctively. Here's how to drive more mindfully. Mindful driving is obviously very different from meditation. You need to keep your eyes open for a start, and rather than focusing inward, you need to be ready to react instantly.

• Before you set off, sit for a minute and breathe in and out. Mentally set your intention for your journey: to be mindful of what is happening.

• Aim to drive with focus – make it your intention to drive smoothly, to accelerate and decelerate gently. Be aware of what is happening ahead, so you are less likely to brake sharply. Stick to the speed limit. These are the best ways to reduce fuel consumption, as well as make the process less stressful.

• Keep the radio or music off so that your attention is solely on the moment. Notice any thoughts of judging that come up, of irritation with bad drivers or unpredictable pedestrians – and let those feelings go.

• Allow your attention to encompass what is happening in the body; be aware of your hands on the wheel, your feet on the pedals, your head shifting to check the mirrors and so on.

• Every time you bring the car to a halt, take the opportunity to notice what is happening in your body and mind. Take a breath, and notice any obvious physical tension points, such as gripping the steering wheel or clenching the jaw. Often simply noticing where we are tense evokes a natural letting-go.

MINDFULNESS AND WORK

Encouraging mindfulness has become a popular corporate tool. Some large companies such as Google and Facebook have set up meditation groups, and such activities are known to help with workplace efficiency.

While corporate support for mindfulness is to be welcomed we should remember that the technique is not for getting ahead at work, it is something that you should do for your own benefit. For many of us, work is where we develop and stretch ourselves most. It is also the source of much of our stress and pressure.

Practicing mindfulness at work can promote a positive perspective on your professional life.

Multi-tasking really means flipping between one task and the other – which is much less efficient

Practising mindfulness can help you to maintain perspective on your professional life. And having a regular meditation can help you to maintain equilibrium when the pressure is on. There are also lots of ways you can bring mindfulness into the working environment.

SINGLE-TASKING

We've become accustomed to think it's good to multi-task. But research shows that the brain can't actually cope with two demanding tasks at once. Multi-tasking really means flipping between one task and the other – which is much less efficient than just concentrating on one thing at a time. So forget about trying to multi-task – and concentrate instead one doing one thing mindfully, then the next, then the one after that…

One simple way to improve your single tasking – and reduce your stress – is to switch off your email alert. A study by the University of London found that people's apparent IQ, as judged by performance, dropped by as much as ten points when they tried to juggle monitoring their emails with their routine tasks. The negative effect was greater than having a terrible night's sleep. And the University of British Columbia found that switching off email alerts and checking emails just three times a day led to a significant reduction in feelings of stress. Interestingly, participants reported that they found it difficult to cut back to three times – a sign that their email checking had become a compulsive habit.

MIND THE GAP

It's easy to get swept up in busyness at work, rushing from one task to the next without a break. But there is always a tiny gap between activities that you can utilise to bring yourself back to a more mindful attitude. Every time you complete something – a report, a phone call, a conversation – take a single breath in and out. Bring your awareness to the body and notice how it feels – are your shoulders tensed up, are you slumping forward. Take a moment to release any unnecessary tension before going back to what you are doing; a few moments with your eyes closed perhaps, or try simply standing up.

PRIORITISE

Keep your to-do list short. If you have a list of things to do that is unachievable, then you are going to spend time worrying about all the undoable things on it. So decide each evening what you are going to accomplish the next day, and limit yourself to a maximum of three things. If you find that difficult, then have two lists: one in which you write down every single thing you have to do, and another in which you write down the three most important things for the next day. When you are working on the most important task, give it your full attention.

REAL LISTENING

When you interact with others, give them your full attention and listen to what is being said. This can also make it easier to accept differences of opinion or criticism. How? Because when we are criticised, many of us feel isolated and angry. Mindfulness practice reminds us to slow down, breathe, and listen to the content of what is being said rather than being swept

Mindfulness practice reminds us to slow down, breathe and listen to the content of what is being said.

up in emotion. It helps us to find the gap between our instinctive reactive emotion (which might be anger or frustration) and the reality of the situation. This means we can choose to respond more calmly and with greater wisdom.

COME BACK TO THE MOMENT

It is much easier to concentrate on the moment if you are feeling calm in your mind. If you are already feeling anxious or stressed, caught up in a torrent of thoughts, it can be more difficult. Here are three ways to come back to the moment.

1 Get physical Bodily sensations can be helpful if you are not able to sit and watch the breath. Try going to the bathroom and wash your hands slowly and deliberately, attending to each action and sensation that you notice. Or pour yourself a glass of

very cold water. Hold the glass and take a sip. Mentally label this action 'sipping'. Try to notice the sensation of coldness as you sip the water.

2 Walk When we are anxious, it is often a good idea to move. So if you can go for a walk – start walking briskly and swing your arms – and gradually slow yourself down when it feels natural to do so.

3 Focus on the feet If you are sitting down and can't easily walk around, then try focusing your attention downward. Bring your attention to your left foot. Start at the big toe and see if you can notice how it feels – are you aware of its position, the gaps between the toes? Slowly focus on the sole of the foot and the sensations that you feel here, then the sides and top, then the ankle.

MINDFUL EATING

In our modern world eating has become a distraction or a source of guilt. We over-eat, under-eat, and worry about eating the wrong things... Mindfulness can help us to reconnect with the pleasure of food.

Eating mindfully is not dieting, or being obsessed with what you eat. It's actually another way of being aware of the moment. It can help identify negative eating habits, and bring you back to the pleasure of food. Here are some ways to bring mindfulness to your mealtimes.

• **Set the scene** Creating a sense of ceremony about your meals can make you appreciate your food more. Make a point of setting the table with cutlery, plates and glasses; try having flowers or candles on the table to create a sense of occasion. Enjoy eating.

• **Use all your senses** Take a moment to notice the look and aromas of your food before you put it in your mouth, perhaps hear the crunch of a nut, or the soft sound when you break a piece of bread. Be aware of the different flavours and where you notice them in the mouth, as well as the feel of the food on your tongue.

• **Eat more slowly** Pause between mouthfuls – setting down your knife and

Mindful eating is not in any way the same as dieting, or obsessing over what you are putting in your mouth. It's actually just another way of being aware of the moment.

fork each time helps to quell the impulse to rush. And chewing your food properly helps you to digest it more easily.

• **Give yourself time** It takes around 20 minutes for the body's feeling of fullness to develop, so eating slowly can help keep you from reaching for a second helping that you do not need. Keep your portions fairly small, having a large amount of food on your plate encourages you to eat more.

• **Be quiet** Eating in silence allows you to concentrate on the act of eating. In monasteries, meals are always taken in silence. If you are eating with other people, a silent meal can be difficult, so perhaps make a point of treating this as a time for good conversation. Try to factor another time for silent eating – perhaps enjoy a peaceful cup of tea each day, or try the mindfulness of eating exercise on page 58.

• **Avoid distractions** Try not to eat in front of the television or laptop. Researchers from the University of Birmingham reviewed studies that looked at how watching a screen at the same time as eating dinner affected how much people ate, and found that not only did watching TV make people eat more, but paying full attention to a meal also led them to eat less later on. Another study found that people who were mentally distracted while they ate or drank needed higher levels of sugar or salt in order to feel satisfied.

• **Give thanks** Many cultures say a few words of appreciation before they start eating. This is a wonderful way to acknowledge one's good fortune in having enough to eat, and this ritual also encourages us to be fully present before we start to eat.

• **When you eat, just eat** Try to avoid eating while you are working or doing something else. If you multi-task you will not appreciate your food fully, and are likely to feel less satisfied. If you are hungry and need to eat, stop and give your snack your full attention.

TRY THIS: THE TEA MEDITATION
However busy you are, there are moments of time in which you can sink into the pleasure of the present moment. Drinking a carefully made, perfect cup of tea can be a beautiful way to practise mindfulness, and is taught by the revered teacher of mindfulness, Vietnamese monk Thich Nhat Hanh. These are the steps to take:

1 Before you start, take a breath. Be aware of the breath as you inhale and you exhale. Know that for this moment there is nothing to do apart from than to be in the present moment.

2 Pick up your cup of tea. Be aware of the heat of the cup, and the weight and feel of it in your hands.

3 Bring the cup to your nose and – without trying to inhale its scent – allow yourself to be aware of the aroma of the tea and the heat of the drink through your nostrils.

4 Now bring the cup to your mouth, noticing how your hand and arm knows exactly where this is without your having to actively think about it. Be aware of any desire to drink the tea – a thought, a watering of the mouth, an instinctive parting of the lips.

5 Notice the feel of the cup on your lip as you prepare to take your sip, and then the feel of the hot tea as it passes into the mouth. Be aware of the flavour of the tea in the mouth. Is it stronger in a particular area of the mouth?

6 Be aware of the act of swallowing – and see if you can notice the impulse to swallow before it occurs.

7 Notice if there is a sense of appreciation as you sip your tea? What form does it take? If you realise that you are lost in thought or have feelings of frustration or other emotions, that's fine – just bring your awareness back to the cup of tea.

8 Allow yourself to finish your cup of tea, enjoying each and every sip as much as the first one. Know that the pleasure of a cup of tea is always available to you, however busy or stressful your day.

A similar mindfulness exercise asks us to bring an awareness of the complex layers of experience contained within a single mouthful of food. This is often done with a single raisin, but you can actually do it with any flavoursome food – a piece of chocolate, a cube of cheese, even a glass of wine or beer.

FLOW ACTIVITIES

We readily bring our full attention to our hobbies and leisure pursuits. When we play sport or do crafts, tend the garden or go climbing, we become absorbed in a way that is naturally akin to mindfulness.

When we are utterly engaged in what we are doing we can feel real joy. A similar state is one that can be attained through meditation and mindfulness – where it is called the 'being' mind – which is very like the experience of being 'in the zone', or what psychologists call 'flow'. When you do a flow activity, you are totally immersed, and body and mind seem to be working in harmony. There is no judging or anticipating, but simply a oneness with the

process. Flow activities are a way that people achieve mindfulness even if they have never heard the term. Athletes may find it when they are racing, joggers when they hit a rhythm and know that they could keep going for hours on end, writers and artists when they get lost in their own creative process.

Flow activities usually have clear goals. They are an enjoyable way to spend time, and they are challenging enough to keep the mind occupied, and they are satisfying because you are in control of your activity rather than having it directed by someone else. Psychologist Mikhail Csíkszentmihály, who first came up with the term 'flow', said that these are the times when people are happiest. Here are some flow activities that may help you to be mindful. Everyone is different, so experiment to see what works for you:

Gardening Studies show that gardening can have the same soothing effects on the body as meditation – including lowered blood pressure and stress, and improved mood. Nurturing plants can give a sense of satisfaction. If you don't have your own

that the rhythm of knitting can have benefits akin to those of meditation. Other textile-based crafts such as sewing, crocheting and cross-stitch can also be flow activities.

Writing Creative writing can be a wonderful way to achieve flow, but you can also get it from keeping a journal. Reading good books can be an immersive experience, too.

garden, try growing indoor plants or a window box – or volunteer to help out in a community garden.

Cooking Preparing food can be a creative activity that can get you in the zone. Try preparing your evening meal mindfully, or giving yourself up to the pleasure of an afternoon of baking.

Exercise Running, golf, yoga, swimming can all be good 'flow' activities.

Art Painting drawing, pottery or colouring – these are all wonderful way to achieve flow. Adult colouring has become hugely popular in recent years, because it can induce a meditative effect without requiring great artistic skill.

Music Singing, dancing or playing an instrument are all by definition activities that have to be done in the present moment, and so can all be great flow activities.

Crafting One study found that knitters reported feeling much happier after knitting, and other studies have suggested

MINDFULNESS OF CHORES

We tend to think of household chores in particular as mindless activities that we deal with as quickly as possibly. But since most of us cannot avoid doing chores, we might as well find a way to make the process engaging.

You can reconfigure your feelings about any activity simply by changing the name of it. Instead of doing the dishes, do the 'doing the dishes meditation'. Instead of making your bed in the morning, embrace your 'mindfulness of making the bed' exercise. Re-labelling something can have a transformative effect on how you feel about it. The very repetitiveness of household chores makes them perfect for

mindfulness practice. More than that, doing chores mindfully can show you that there is real joy in simple activities, that each moment of life is worth living. It allows you to be more conscious of the sense of achievement when a task has been well done, and is complete, and to enjoy the doing of it.

If a chore is one that you truly dislike – cleaning the bathroom, or ironing shirts –

then this is also a valuable way to practise acceptance. We all have to spend time doing things that we dislike, so we delay, complain, or get upset about it. This makes it much harder to do – it is the second arrow of suffering discussed on pages 28–9. Practising tolerance in our own time allows us to build our ability to accept the things that we cannot change.

So the 'mindfulness of chores' can help get you in touch with your own resistance when things are not as you wish them to be. And it can help you to build an ability to tolerate and accept imperfections in your experience. If you live with other people or have children, then doing mindful chores together can be a pleasurable activity and a way of teaching your children to embrace acceptance.

You can do any chore mindfully. Try folding the laundry. Before you start take a moment to breathe and to check in with your body. What can you feel? Are you aware of any sense of annoyance or

impatience? What thoughts are arising? 'This is pointless', 'I will get this done and then have a nice cup of tea'? Just notice what is there.

Look at the pile of clothes in front of you. Then begin folding the first item slowly. As you bring all of your focus to the task, notice the colours of the clothes, how the light falls on them, the feel of the fabric under your fingers, and the scent of the washing powder. Fold with care, noticing how your hands and arms move to achieve this. Experience fully the act of placing each folded item in the pile. Try to fold the laundry as if you have never folded laundry before – with the beginner's mind.

At the end of the task, take another moment to look at your pile of neat laundry, and acknowledge the fact that you have used this time to practise mindfulness. Consider how you feel, and whether the activity felt different to normal.

Practising tolerance in our own time allows us to build our ability to accept the things that we cannot change.

FINDING CUES

It is difficult to stay mindful every moment throughout the day. So it can be helpful to build reminders into the routine of your daily round. Whenever you encounter one of these cues, you will be prompted to be mindful.

We are constantly contactable: we have lost the possibility of solitude, but also perhaps the habit of being completely present in the company of others.

The more often we can have a moment of mindfulness, the more likely we are to build up a pervasive attitude of mindfulness that can carry us through the day. Here are some techniques designed to prompt you to check in with yourself.

The phone It is a fact of modern life that many of us have become used to being constantly contactable: we have lost the possibility of solitude, but also perhaps the habit of being completely present in the company of others. When the phone rings, don't jump to answer it immediately – or if you receive the beep of a new text or message, treat it as a signal to take one breath in and one breath out.

Something you wear If there is an item of jewellery or a watch that you wear every day, then you could decide that this is going to be your mindfulness reminder. Every time you catch sight of that ring or bracelet or wristwatch, take a moment's pause: are you aware of what you are doing? How is your body feeling? How is your breath?

Ring the bell You can download a mindfulness reminder onto your computer that will chime every hour (or whenever you set it) – just search for 'mindfulness bell'. When this sounds, use it as a reminder to check in with yourself – how does your body feel in this moment? – or to breathe, or to get up and walk around.

Passing through Doorways are an excellent cue to mindfulness. In the course of any day, you are likely to pass through many doorways or entrances. As you cross any threshold, simply be aware that you are passing from one space to another, and take note of where you are mentally as well as physically.

Boiling the kettle If making a cup of tea or coffee is how you take a break, the time that the kettle is boiling, or the coffee pot is percolating can seem like dead time. It doesn't need to be: this is the perfect opportunity to practise some mindful breathing until your drink is ready.

Take a seat We sit down and then get up again numerous times during the day. Make a point of paying attention to the process of sitting and standing – if you forget, take a moment to notice the feeling of the chair underneath you, and the ground beneath your feet.

POWERING DOWN

In recent years it has become more difficult than ever to spend our time mindfully, because the proliferation of electronic devices has meant that there is always a way to escape our present.

Most of us are probably using our smartphones a lot more than we think. One 2015 survey by Nottingham Trent and other universities found that users checked their phones 85 times a day. Using your smartphone isn't a problem in itself, of course, but the study found that users checked their phones twice as often as they thought they did. In other words, it had become a mindless habit they were unaware of.

Mobile devices are of course brilliant and useful pieces of technology. It would be wrong – not to say futile and absurd – to condemn them as one of the evils of modern life. Nevertheless, it is possible to become addicted to checking your phone, or to the buzz that we get when a message comes in, or when a post is liked or 'favourited'. There is one other way in which your mobile or tablet can be a barrier to mindfulness. The phone is

always in reach, and that means that there is always something that we can fill our thoughts with, rather than be still. It is, in other words, one of the ways that we can keep our minds in an empty 'doing' mode rather than switch into 'being'.

Now, nobody is telling you to throw away your phone. But do take a look at these ways of restricting your usage, so that your online presence doesn't become a mindless habit.

• Think when you use your phone most. Is it when you are bored, or lonely? Is there something more productive or worthwhile that you could do instead?

• Go to your phone settings and turn off all the separate alerts for incoming texts, emails, and social media notifications. Alternatively, when you hear a text alert treat this as a cue for mindfulness. Take a conscious breath in and out before looking at your phone.

> *The phone is always in reach, and that means that there is always something that we can fill our thoughts with, rather than be still.*

• Make a decision about when you do not want to use your phone – in bed, when you are playing with your children, when you watch TV. Stick to it – put the phone in a different room.

• If you continually check your phone for emails and updates, give yourself set times to check it – three times a day, or once an hour. If that feels too hard, start by limiting yourself to 15-minute intervals, then 30, then hourly.

• Have phone-free zones in your home – the dinner table, the bedroom, or the living room. It's also a good idea to have a cut-off point after which you won't check your phone – 9pm, say.

• Go cold turkey, and delete the apps that you waste most time on – or anything that is a non-essential.

AND SO TO BED

One in three people has some difficulty sleeping. Bringing mindfulness to your evening can be an effective way to alleviate sleep problems, and it can make for a more enjoyable evening, too.

Most adults need seven to nine hours sleep a night, but sixty per cent of us get less than that. One reason is that we simply go to bed too late. So, as a first step, work out what time you need to get up and work backwards to establish what time you should go to bed. If you set your alarm for 6am, then it will help to know you ought to be in bed by 11pm at the latest.

Sleep experts advise us to stick to the same sleep schedule, including at weekends. This won't always be feasible, but try to keep the same hours as far as possible. And it is worth reminding yourself that your sleep routine begins before lights-out. You won't be asleep at 11 if you work or watch TV until five to. Here are some ways to prepare for your night's rest.

1 Have an evening 'slow-down' call. Set a clock or your phone to sound a couple of hours before you need to be asleep. Treat this as the signal to begin winding down.

2 Be aware of the reasons that you find to stay up late. They are often pretty flimsy – like watching a programme that we could quite easily miss, or record.

3 Don't use electronic devices within two hours of bedtime. They emit light that suppresses the body's production of the sleep hormone melatonin.

4 If you can, dim the lights before bedtime. Most bathrooms have bright lighting so try just using the mirror light when brushing your teeth, or do it in the dark.

5 Follow a ritual. Doing the same things before bed each day, at the same time, helps to prime you for sleep – a nightly

Mindfulness and sleep

A study conducted by the Stanford Medical Centre discovered that participants in its six-week programme of mindfulness and meditation found that they got to sleep twice as quickly as before. This may be because mindfulness helps people to combat the worries that so often surface in those wakeful minutes, and keep people from finding sleep.

warm bath and a hot drink, for example, which also helps your body to reach the optimum temperature for rest. Or you could do a meditation or calming yoga practice. Do these things with care and attention, the mindful way.

6 Avoid any kind of mental or emotional excitement or mental stimulation (such as computer games) or difficult conversations.

Anything that gets your adrenaline pumping is bad for sleep.

7 Once you are in bed – or if you wake up in the middle of the night – do the body scan or mindfulness of breathing (see pages 96–8 and 82–5). You can also count the number of sounds that you can hear. If you can't sleep, give in to the situation; accept it rather than resist it.

mindfulness
MEDITATION

MEDITATION PRACTICE

Mindfulness is not quite the same thing as meditation, though they are related. Mindfulness is paying attention to what we are doing – it is a way of living. In meditation, we pay attention to the experience of non-doing.

There are many reasons to meditate, but perhaps the most important benefit is that meditation allows us to get to know ourselves better. When we take the time simply to be, we are able to observe our thoughts, feelings, and the sensations of the body without distraction. This creates

When we take the time simply to be, we are able to observe our thoughts, feelings, and the sensations of the body without distraction.

Meditation effects

Mindfulness meditation is a gentle yet powerful technique with positive benefits. It can sometimes, however, bring up strong negative emotions or difficult memories. There are various ways to work with these but if you feel overwhelmed, then it is best to stop the meditation and seek advice from your doctor or from an experienced therapist or mindfulness teacher.

Pictures of meditators often show them with a slight smile. It's not just because they are blissed out – though they may well be having a wonderful time – but because bringing the mouth into a smile helps to release tension from the face.

a sense of spaciousness in our mind, which not only helps to bring us to a calmer state but also allows us greater clarity and understanding of who we are and of what drives our actions. In short, a regular meditation practice increases our capacity to be mindful in daily life.

There are different forms of meditation – but in mindfulness meditation the point is simply to notice what is happening right now, with an attitude of gentle curiosity and kindness. We start by using breath as a way of anchoring ourselves to each moment as it unfolds, but we can also choose to pay attention to other aspects of our experience as we receive them through our senses.

You don't need equipment to meditate – or anything much at all. But your body temperature tends to drop if you are still for any length of time, so you might want to have a shawl or thin blanket that you can put around your shoulders to keep warm. It's obviously good to be wearing clothing that does not restrict your movements, especially if you are sitting on the floor and need to bend your knees. You may need a cushion or two to help you sit comfortably (see page 78–81 for advice on postures), and it may help to have some kind of alarm clock or app on your phone, so that you don't become distracted by constantly checking what the time is. (It is also generally a good idea to decide how long you are going to meditate for before you start.)

It is good to be in a quiet place where you will not be disturbed. This can be outside or indoors, whatever suits you best. Many people find it helpful to meditate in the same place each day. Keeping your meditation space uncluttered can also be helpful so you are not distracted by extraneous objects, or by the thought that you really should tidy up. Be sure to turn off your phone or leave it somewhere else.

MAKING TIME FOR MEDITATION

A short daily practice can give you a sense of space in a busy day, but many of us feel pressed for time. It's true that trying to 'fit in' meditation can be a challenge, but perhaps the best solution is to change the way you look at it.

When considering how to fit a meditation practice into your daily routine, think about the things that you do make time for. If, say, you watch TV for a couple of hours each night, then you cannot really tell yourself that you don't have time for a few minutes' meditation. One way to approach this conversation with yourself is to try to notice the impulse to watch TV. You don't have to stop yourself – just notice the urge and be aware of the act of switching on the TV. Say 'I am choosing to watch TV right now'. Now think about whether you have time for meditation. It is healthier and

Make it easy for yourself. You can do a minute's meditation practice each day – pick a time just after doing something else; for example, when you first get out of bed.

more honest to say 'I do not want to meditate, I want to watch TV' than it is to say 'I do not have time to meditate'. If your schedule really is very busy, it can be stressful to open your mind to another thing 'to do' – and meditation or yoga can sometimes feel like just another chore.

Try to notice this attitude of making everything into a job – is there a different way of looking at it? Make it easy for yourself. You can do a minute's meditation each day – pick a time just after doing something else; for example, when you first get out of bed. Or be clear about the fact that you are not going to do formal practice right now, but will concentrate on bringing your meditation into everyday living – for example, that you will clear the table mindfully each day. There are lots of ideas about how to do this in the previous chapter.

Or just do it! If you want to discover what mindfulness can mean for you, then make a commitment to practise. Write it on your calendar, drop some of your plans or other commitments, stop watching the TV. The fact is: you do have time for five minutes, you can make that space in your day. So you could just resolve to make it happen. Sometimes we need to give ourselves a firm but gentle push to get started.

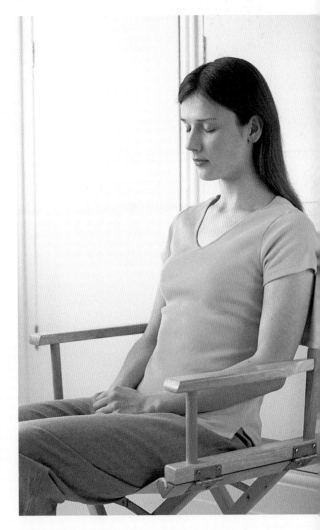

BUILD YOUR PRACTICE

Here are some tips and techniques to help your practice to take root and grow.

Start tiny Make a goal that is not just easily achievable, but laughably so. Rather than deciding to meditate for 20 minutes a day, go for just 30 seconds. Once you have done that every day for a week or two, increase to a minute or five minutes and so on.

Do it early Meditating early in the day is a good idea – not only because it gets it done, but also because it helps put you in a mindful mood for the rest of the day.

Tag it It's easy to remember to meditate if you link it to something else you do each day. Do it as soon as you have had your morning cup of tea, for example.

Or set an alarm Programme your mobile to sound a chime at a set time each day, or write your meditation on your daily to-do list if you have one.

Commit to it Decide that you are going to do your meditation each day, and just do it. If you think you are too busy, then examine what you mean by that. Anyone has time for a simple one minute's meditation no matter how much they have to fit in to their day.

Set out your stall If you use anything for meditation – a particular corner of a room, shawl, the right cushions – keep it all in one place. Then when it is time, you can sit down and get started.

Know why you are doing it Think about why you want to meditate. Is there a key benefit that resonates with you – perhaps a wish to be less irritable. Write down, 'I want to meditate because…' on a piece of paper and put it somewhere safe. Get it out and look at it when you waver.

Be self-kind If you miss the odd day, don't give yourself a hard time. Simply start anew the next day. Or if you miss a morning session, do it later in the day.

Have trust Keep going with your meditation even if you think it is not working. Deciding that you will continue practising for a set period – however it feels – is important because we don't always feel an instant sense of peace. Sometimes meditation is difficult, boring or frustrating, and the benefits may not be apparent. We have to trust it is worthwhile.

Set targets It's often said that it takes 21 days to form a new habit, but this is a myth. You need to make a continual effort to maintain a habit. You are more likely to continue with meditation if you accept this.

Make a note Write down what you want to do on a piece of paper – 'I am going to meditate at 8am each day for five minutes.' Put this somewhere you will see it. Conversely if you want to miss your meditation for some reason, make a point of writing this down – 'I am missing my meditation today because…' Our reason may be spurious, and the act of writing it down can help us see that.

GET COMFORTABLE

There are four basic positions used in meditation: sitting, lying down, standing and walking. No one posture is intrinsically better, but whatever posture you choose, it is important to be comfortable.

The key thing is to be able to sit without discomfort – if you feel a lot of pain, then it is hard to concentrate on the breath.

SITTING POSTURES

Most people meditate while they are sitting. It is easier to keep alert in this position than when lying down, and it is less strenuous than standing. When we think of meditation, we often imagine people sitting on the floor, cross-legged or in the lotus position. Most of us, however, don't spend much time sitting on the floor as adults and so we find it unfamiliar and perhaps uncomfortable. If this is the case, it is fine to sit on a chair or to kneel. The key thing is to be able to sit without discomfort – if you feel a lot of pain, then it is hard to concentrate on the breath. However you sit, rest your hands on your thighs or your lap (perhaps on a cushion) to allow the shoulders to relax. If you feel discomfort between the shoulders, you may need a higher cushion.

Sitting on a chair Choose a chair that has a straight back and a slightly cushioned seat, like a dining chair, rather than a soft armchair or sofa. If you can, sit with your bottom on the centre of the seat so that you sit upright rather than slouching or leaning back. If this is too difficult, then place a cushion between your bottom and the back of the chair to encourage a more upright posture.

Have your feet flat on the floor, roughly shoulder-width apart, and your hips slightly higher than your knees (this tilts the pelvis forwards, which helps to keep your back straight); you may need to place a cushion under your bottom or under your feet to achieve this. Bring your chin very slightly towards the chest to elongate the spine to its full extent.

Sitting on the floor Sitting cross-legged on the floor tilts the pelvis backwards making it difficult to keep the spine straight. It's better to bend the legs and place one calf in front of the other; this is known as the Burmese position. Place a cushion under your bottom and sit on the front third of it; this brings your pelvis forward. It's most comfortable if the knees rest on the floor; if yours don't reach, then place a cushion or two under each knee.

You will become more flexible over time, and it is a good idea to alternate the legs each time you meditate, so you build your flexibility evenly. You can buy cushions specially designed for sitting meditation (called zafus).

Kneeling Some people find kneeling more comfortable than sitting. You can get a special kneeling bench – called a seiza bench – to keep your weight off your feet, or you can sit astride a firm pillow folded in half. It can also help to place a rolled blanket or towel under your ankles. Rather than kneel on a hard floor, it is best to kneel on a wide flat cushion (called a zabuton) or on a folded blanket.

LYING DOWN POSTURE

If you find it hard to sit or kneel, then you can meditate lying down. There is a compelling temptation to fall asleep, but if you have back pain or other problems that make sitting painful then lying down may

STANDING POSTURE

Many people do not like to stand still for any period of time, but learning to stand motionless can help build patience and body-knowledge, as well as stamina.

Standing meditation is traditionally taught in Buddhist practice alongside sitting, lying down and walking meditation. It helps with posture and balance, and can create a deep sense of calm in the body. If you are feeling sleepy in sitting meditation, standing up can wake you up. Standing meditation can also be a useful thing to do when you are just waiting – for your children to come out of school, in the checkout queue, for a bus.

Most of us do not stand well – we lean onto one side or the other, so it can feel difficult to stand comfortably for long periods. Here is how to find a comfortable standing position. Start with one minute the first time you try standing meditation, and gradually build up the time.

be the best position for you. Meditating in this position can also be a lovely thing to do last thing at night, while you are in bed. For most people, the most comfortable position is lying on your back with your legs hip-width apart, and your knees bent so that the soles of your feet flat are on the floor. Rest your head on a thin cushion or folded towel. Alternatively, you can also lie on your side with your knees bent and bending your arm so that you can rest your head in your hand.

1 Stand with your feet hip-width to shoulder-width apart and your arms by your side. Bend your knees slightly to prevent them from locking.

2 Rock slowly back and forth from your heels to the balls of your feet. Slow the rocking down gradually, and come to a stop in a position that feels neither forwards or backwards.

3 Round your shoulders forwards and then bring them back a few times, and then pause in a position that feels neither forwards nor backwards, but central.

4 Imagine that a piece of string is attached to your head lifting it upwards. Keep your neck relaxed and your chin slightly tilted towards the chest. This brings the head in line with the spine.

5 Half close the eyes and fix your gaze on a point that is a metre or so in front of you. Your gaze should be soft.

MINDFULNESS OF BREATHING

In mindfulness meditation the breath is the focus. We notice the breath passing into and out of the body. It sounds so simple – and it is – but watching the breath can also be a profound and life-changing experience.

Breathing is both a conscious and an unconscious activity. It is something that happens without our needing to manage it – but at any given moment we can take control and choose to deepen our breath or make it shallower, lengthen or shorten it, slow it down or speed it up. But when we meditate, we are not trying to control our breathing; rather, we are observing the breath just as it is in this moment.

Paying attention to the breath allows us to see how the mind leaps from one thought to another – sometimes referred to as the 'monkey mind'. Mindful breathing also helps us with the detached observation of emotions – how, when we practise, they can rise up in the body and then pass without our getting caught up in them. And, since our breathing changes depending on our posture, our activity and

But when we meditate, we are not trying to control our breathing in any way; rather, we are observing the breath just as it is in this moment.

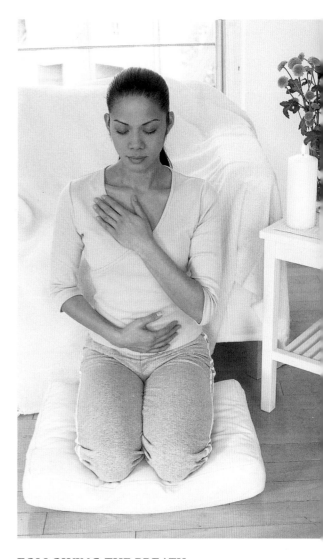

our emotion, learning to notice the breath teaches us a great deal about what we are doing and how we are feeling.

It is important to remember that although our focus is observing the breath, our intention is simply to pay attention in a non-judgemental and kindly manner. So even if we lose our focus many, many times, we can maintain our intention by gently and uncritically directing our attention back to the breath every time.

Help your focus

It can be helpful to count the breath when you start. Breathe in and breathe out, and silently count 'one'. Keep counting until you reach ten, and then start again. You may not get past 'one' before you become distracted. That's okay. Just start again… and again… and again. When you feel ready, stop counting and just watch the breath.

FOLLOWING THE BREATH

Once you have settled in a comfortable posture – sitting, kneeling, lying down or standing – close your eyes and mouth (so you breathe through the nostrils).

1 Allow yourself to notice the passage of the breath, wherever you are most aware of it in the body.

• **at the nostrils** when you breathe in, you may notice the slight coldness of air passing into the nostrils, and when you breathe out you may feel the breath, warmer now, as it passes out. This is a very subtle sensation, so you need to be able to bring a delicacy of attention in order to feel it.

• **at the chest** you may find it easier to notice the breath in the chest area, which expands and rises as you inhale and contracts and falls again when you exhale. Try taking a deep breath in, to help you become aware of this movement. You may be able to feel the lungs pressing, 'against the back of the ribcage' as you inhale.

• **in the belly** when you are relaxed, your abdomen expands as you breathe in, and contracts when you breathe out. This may be where you notice the breath most. Again, taking a deep breath in can help you to notice this – try placing a hand softly on your belly as you do so.

2 When you have decided where you feel the breath most keenly, then stick with this as your focus throughout the meditation. If they all feel noticeable to you, then just pick one area and stick with that.

3 Remember that you are not trying to breathe particularly deeply or smoothly, or trying to relax (though that is often a nice side-effect of meditation). The intention is simply to explore how it feels to follow the breath – being mindful of what is in this moment. Think of it as an experiment to discover the difference between being (noticing the breath) and doing (controlling the breath). This can be much harder than it sounds, so don't worry if you keep noticing yourself trying to breathe in a particular way; keep gently bringing the attention back to noticing, noticing, always noticing.

4 Our minds are not used to focusing on our breathing, so you may find you lose concentration very quickly. That's fine. As soon as you notice that you have become

Attending to the gap can engender a deep sense of relaxation as your awareness rests on a moment when the body is utterly still.

distracted, gently direct your attention back to your breathing. There is no need to judge or criticise yourself for this – that's just another distraction. But if you find yourself feeling annoyed with yourself or unhappy that you lose concentration so often, don't then criticise yourself for that. And come to that, don't start criticising yourself for the fact that you are criticising yourself. Whatever point you are at, pause and direct your attention back to the breath.

5 Continue concentrating on the breath for the time you have set – two minutes, five minutes, 30 minutes or whatever. At the end of the meditation, open your eyes and get up slowly – there is no rush.

GOING FURTHER

Mindfulness of breathing is a useful anchor to any meditation session. You can continue with mindfulness of breathing throughout the meditation, or you can use it as a starting point to help you settle into a more aware state and then go on to practise mindfulness of body sensations, of sound or thoughts and feelings. The meditations on pages 86–94 work with the mindfulness of breath, and are often taught consecutively.

As you become more aware of your breathing, you will realise just how rich the experience of a single moment can be – each breath can be shallow or deep, ragged or smooth, fast or slow – so different. One beautiful thing you may start to notice is that there is a tiny gap at the end of each in-breath – a moment when you are neither breathing in nor breathing out – and another tiny gap at the end of each out-breath. Try focusing your attention on this gap without trying to force it or elongate it. Attending to the gap can engender a deep sense of relaxation as your awareness rests on a moment when the body is utterly still.

MINDFUL BODY MEDITATION

Bodily sensations are another aspect of our experience that we can use as an object of focus in meditation. Practising awareness of physical sensations helps us to be grounded in the body and to broaden our awareness.

Observing our physical sensations enables us to become more aware of the interplay between mind and body. If, for example, you notice a sensation of aching in your shoulder, you may also notice an associated feeling of irritation that an old injury is playing up, and then the thought that this shoulder is not as flexible as it should be. You may find yourself going into a narrative about how you got this injury, and all the things this shoulder can and cannot now do...

In the following mindful body meditation, we are aware of our thoughts and feelings, but we keep our attention on the physical sensation.

1 Take a comfortable but alert position on the floor or a chair, and close your eyes. Bring your attention to wherever your body makes contact with the floor or chair. Spend a little time noticing the physical sensations you experience here – what do you feel?

2 Spend a minute or two focusing on the breath as it comes into the body and out of the body.

3 Then, if a feeling or sensation in the body pulls at your attention, give it your focus. Notice what you are experiencing here without judging it as pleasant or unpleasant, and without either mentally pushing it away or trying to hold on to it. Try to be open to it with an attitude of curiosity: is this sensation cold or warm or burning, is there a feeling of tingling, twisting or aching? Is it a fixed sensation or does it in fact change and move in subtle ways?

4 Remember that you do not have to do anything to alter what you are experiencing; the aim is simply to observe it. As thoughts or emotions come up, be aware of them but, as much as you are able, keep your focus on the sensation you are investigating.

5 When the sensation passes or ceases to hold your attention, then let your focus move back to the breath until another body sensation presents itself. Alternatively, if your attention is drawn to another elsewhere in the body, let your focus shift there.

6 The quality of your attention should be light, rather than forced. If a sensation feels very intense, then do not grit your teeth as if you are participating in a test of endurance. Maintaining a still position is useful in meditation, but not if you are experiencing pain. It is fine to move to find a greater sense of ease if you need to, but do so deliberately and slowly. This is a very different activity than constant fidgeting or reacting the second you feel something uncomfortable, and is just a small and thoughtful favour that you are doing for yourself.

7 At the end of the meditation, open your eyes. Get up slowly, maintaining your awareness of your body as you do so. This may be a good moment to check in with the needs of the physical self – perhaps you want to stretch or feel like going for a walk.

MINDFUL SOUND MEDITATION

Sound is ever-present. If you pause just for a moment and listen, you will immediately become aware of sound all around you. This meditation helps you differentiate between the sound itself and the act of hearing.

1 Take a comfortable position in a quiet place where you will not be disturbed, and gently close your eyes. Spend a minute or two becoming aware of the breath as it flows in and out of the body, to help root yourself in the moment.

2 When you feel ready, allow your awareness to open up to the sounds around you.

3 Notice sounds wherever they come from – far away or close by, behind you or in front of you, to your left or right, above you

or beneath you. Be open both to loud sounds – a sudden cough or person talking outside the window – and to the ambient sounds – the slight wind in the trees outside, the whisper of a radiator.

4 There is a difference between receiving sound and consciously listening out for it. In this exercise, you are aiming to notice the act of hearing itself; you are not

actively hunting for sounds to listen to. So allow sounds to flow in, as if your ears were mere receptacles for noises. You may be able to notice the different stages of a sound: its arising, its presence, and its fading away.

5 When we perceive sound, our minds classify it as 'birdsong', 'vacuum cleaner', 'humming' or whatever. This is a different process to receiving the sound itself – receiving the sound is a passive act (being) whereas naming it is an activity of the mind (doing). What is more, we are not succeeding in merely receiving when we notice that a sound is pleasant (birdsong) or unpleasant (an ambulance siren), because that perception involves the additional act of judging. As best you can, let go of the need to classify and judge, and try to experience the sensation of the sound just as it is. You may find this experience elusive: you may find yourself 'hearing' for a moment so brief that you barely notice it before you are 'listening' again. It takes practise.

6 When you notice that you have become distracted by naming, judging, or by a story in your mind, gently come back to sound. If you feel that you have lost concentration altogether, then you can return to the breath at any point.

Mindful hearing
Sound is wave movement. Vibrations in the air make parts of the inner ear move – just as the flow of a river makes the wheel of a watermill turn. A waterwheel, bear in mind, is not making an effort to turn – its movement is in a sense entirely passive; it is natural and unforced. And you need not make an effort when you are hearing mindfully. Allow the sounds simply to flow into your consciousness and out again, like running water.

THOUGHT AWARENESS MEDITATION

Learning to be aware of our thoughts without getting carried away by them can be a useful technique for stress release. This meditation is best done in conjunction with mindfulness of breathing.

It's not easy to be a dispassionate observer of your own thoughts. Any thought can be the spark of some narrative of worry or fantasy, and we may spend much of our time lost in these tales that we tell to ourselves. Imagine that you see someone eating an ice cream, for example. Depending on who you are, this may lead you to embark on a whole reverie of nostalgia, or it may lead you into a troublesome stream of thoughts about your weight. Some of our inner storytelling

Planned thoughts

If you have a recurring worry or thought, it can help to make a time when you will address it. Decide that you will think about this issue at, say, 6pm that evening – or at noon on Saturday. Then every time it comes up in your mind, remind yourself that you have an appointment to think about it and that you will save it and wait until then.

Observing your thoughts without getting caught up in them can help you to realise that your thoughts do not define you.

may be pleasurable, and some of it may be deeply wounding, But all of it tends to take us away from the present moment. It doesn't have to be like this. Thoughts – like sounds – can arise, be present and then pass. Observing your thoughts

The labelling technique

Putting a name to a thought or feeling is a mindfulness technique that helps to create a sense of space between the thoughts and feelings on the one hand, and the person experiencing them on the other. This is to remind us that we are not defined by our thoughts and feelings, which are temporary and fleeting states of mind. What is more, a thought or feeling can be observed but does not need to be believed: we need not let them overwhelm us.

Labelling trains us to acknowledge an aspect of our experience, and to let it go rather than getting caught up in it. Psychological research has found that simply recognising a thought or feeling and giving it a name lessens its effect on us.

Labelling is intended to be a simple thing, so beware the tendency to over-focus on it. The aim is to notice what is happening and then to give it a label. You do not want to spend time or effort on coming up with the exact label, or to label everything that happens. Keep your attention light, and don't worry if you cannot come up with a name for something, or if the label comes up after the thought or feeling has already passed. When you start

using labelling, it is much easier to use general categories ('thinking', say) rather than more precise definitions ('planning' or 'remembering'). And do remember the key thing is to notice. If you find yourself criticising your labelling technique, then label this 'thinking'. If you find labelling distracts you from the process of noticing, then it is fine not to use the technique.

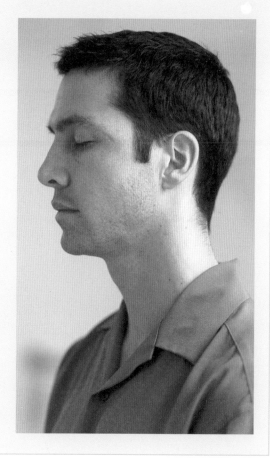

without getting caught up in them can help you to realise that your thoughts do not define you. You are not the sum of what you think. Understanding this gives you a valuable tool that can release you from negative cycles of anxiety or empty daydreaming. The following meditation should help you develop the ability to observe your thoughts and feelings.

1 Start with a short period of mindfulness of breathing, to help settle yourself into the meditation, and then expand your awareness into mindfulness of sounds – noticing as sounds begin, are present and then pass away, being aware of the constant changes in their qualities.

2 Then, as you breathe naturally, gently slide your awareness to whatever is arising in the mind. At first it may seem as if there is nothing happening. There is no need to try and generate thoughts; simply observe the quietness of your mind. Sooner or later, you will catch one – even if the thought is 'I'm not thinking anything.'

3 When you notice a thought, observe it – you can label it 'thinking' if it helps – letting it dissolve of its own accord, and watching the next thought rise like a bubble.

4 You will almost certainly find yourself distracted by some thoughts – you may realise all of a sudden that you are lost in some story or perhaps reliving an unpleasant memory. As soon as you notice, turn your attention back to observing your thoughts again – using the label 'thinking' if it helps.

5 Thoughts can be like ocean waves. You might want to dive in among them, or you may find them frightening and forceful. Perhaps you get carried off in a current of thoughts. If that happens, simply bring yourself back to your focus as soon as you are able. You cannot stop a wave from forming, but you can ride it or let it move on by you while you stay more or less still.

6 If you feel overwhelmed by your thoughts or if you find yourself unable to focus, then you can observe the breath or sounds to bring yourself back to the moment. When your mind feels steady, you can return to observing your thoughts if you feel able. It takes time to develop your ability to observe your thoughts, so do not push yourself further than you feel willing to go.

7 When you feel ready, turn your attention to your feelings. Emotions can be triggered by or associated with body sensations, our thoughts, or our state of mind; they may be pleasant (happiness,

peace) or unpleasant (anger, boredom). Whatever feelings are present in the body, try to open up to them without either pushing them away or, conversely, trying to get more of them.

8 Feelings, like thoughts or body sensations, are continually arising, being present and then passing. Try to observe the feeling, noticing how and where you are experiencing it in the body.

9 Be aware of any thoughts that are associated with the feeling you've observed. Remember that the quality of your investigation should be light and curious but also compassionate – if a feeling feels difficult or too intense, then return your focus back to the breath to study yourself. Sometimes following the path of a feeling, however, and allowing it to pass, can give you an insight into its temporary nature.

Choiceless awareness

This is a more advanced meditation that you can practise once you are familiar with the mindfulness of the breath, body, sound, thoughts and feelings

exercises. In choiceless awareness, rather than focusing on one object of focus at a time, you allow the mind to focus on whatever is most compelling in this moment – whether that is the breath, thoughts, feelings, bodily sensations or sounds.

Try it for a few minutes, simply being aware of whatever is uppermost in your experience and then letting it go as something else occurs. You may find that you become lost in thought more quickly than if you are concentrating on a specific object (such as the breath). If so, the labelling technique (see page 91) can be helpful. Or you can simply come back to focusing on the breath for a few moments and then allow your awareness to broaden out again when your mind feels steady.

THE BODY SCAN

This is a different type of mindfulness exercise that invites you to explore the sensations of the body gently and systematically, from your feet to your face. It takes 20–30 minutes, so do it when you will not be disturbed.

This exercise is taught as a way of connecting with your physical self and developing a greater awareness of the sensations of the body. When we feel pain or discomfort, we generally try either to ignore it or fix it, but there is evidence to show that accepting uncomfortable sensations can help to relieve or reduce pain and tension in the body.

In this exercise, we take a tour around the body. We notice, with a sense of compassion and acceptance, what is happening to our physical self. This can lead to a deep sense of relaxation and reconnection with the body.

1 Lie down in a comfortable position, and cover yourself with a blanket if necessary, to prevent yourself from getting cold; your body temperature may drop when you lie still for a lengthy period. You can do this exercise lying on the floor, or on your bed, wherever you feel relaxed and where you won't be disturbed. Close your eyes.

2 Notice where your body makes contact with the surface beneath you. Allow the floor (or bed) to take your weight – there is no need to hold yourself up. It can help to imagine yourself dropping down into the surface beneath you as you exhale, a little further each time.

3 As you relax, spend a minute or two paying attention to the breath wherever you notice it most – at the nostrils, in the chest area, or in the belly area – to help yourself settle into the meditation. Remember to be with the breath just as it is, without trying to change it.

4 Now gently bring your awareness to your toes – how do they feel? Perhaps there is a sense of coldness or warmth, tingling, aching or tension. If you are wearing socks you may be aware of the contact with the fabric, the toes touching each other, their contours – even the spaces between them. As you breathe in and out, notice what you feel with an attitude of acceptance and non-judgement. And if you feel nothing at all, accept this nothingness as the thing that you are feeling.

5 Allow your awareness to glide to the soles of your feet, including the ball and the heel, and explore them in the same

When we feel pain or discomfort, we generally try either to ignore it or fix it, but there is evidence to show that accepting uncomfortable sensations can help to relieve or reduce pain and tension in the body.

way. Start with a general awareness of the area as a whole and as a sensation comes to your attention, allow yourself to focus on it for a deeper exploration of its qualities. It is as if your awareness were a kind of butterfly on the wing, seeking out a spot in which to land.

6 When you are ready, move on to the top and sides of the foot, investigating what you can feel here and being present with any discomfort, as best as you can right now. As you attend to each area, letting the previous one fade from your consciousness.

7 Move your attention upward to the ankle, calf and shin, knee and thigh, continuing to breathe in and out. Of course, your attention will wander from time to time, and you may become lost in your thoughts. Just gently bring your focus back to the area you are exploring. If it helps, use the labelling technique for the area that you are exploring 'foot, shin etc'.

8 Now bring your attention into the bottom, to the pelvis and hips and from here travel up the body, scanning each part in turn. As you explore the abdomen and the chest, notice how they move with your in-breath and out-breath. You may be aware of pulsation or movement deep inside the body. You may even notice the movement of the heart as it beats. Just be aware of what is happening in this moment, allowing whatever sensations you experience to be as they are.

9 Then scan your arms, starting with the tips of your fingers and working your way up to the shoulders. From here, scan the neck and throat, noticing any tension and allowing it to release naturally.

10 Move on to the head, and scan each part of the head and face in turn – notice the head as a whole, and gently direct your attention from jaw to forehead to crown, ear to ear, the face to the back of the head. When a sensation tugs at your attention, allow your awareness to rest on it as it changes and dissolves, or another sensation becomes more compelling. Be patient: what you feel is what you feel, whether there are many sensations or few.

11 Finally, allow yourself to expand your awareness outwards, from one part of the body to the whole. Be aware of the breath as it passes into the body and out again, but keep your focus general and open until you feel the meditation is at an end.

Breathing into the body

A variation of the body scan involves directing the breath to whatever area you are scanning – as if you are breathing into your toes, say, and out of your toes. All you do is follow the breath as it passes into the body and then imagine it travelling through, say, the leg and foot into the toes.

At the same time as you breathe out, you imagine that the exhalation originates in the toes and then travels back through the body. This type of visualisation can encourage a gentle natural releasing of any tension that is held in the area of the body you are working with.

WALKING MEDITATION

Meditative walking is a wonderful way of honing your awareness and developing a sense of connectedness with the world. You can practise mindful walking at any time but this exercise is a more formal undertaking.

Walking meditation involves pacing back and forth along a short set area, attending to the sensations of the feet and lower legs. This kind of meditation practice can be a good way to focus the mind if you are prone to feeling sleepy during sitting meditation, and it can also be a good way to occupy the mind if you tend to feel restless or uncomfortable when sitting. You can vary your pace according to your

mood – if you are feeling restless, for example then you may like to start with brisk walking meditation, whereas very slow walking may feel more appropriate if you are already feeling calm.

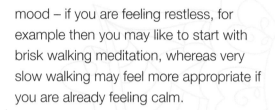

1 Choose a place that is reasonably flat and about 6–10m long. This can be in your garden or in a quiet area of a park, or it can be indoors: in a hallway, say.

2 Stand at one end of the space. Relax your shoulders, bring your palms together in the namaste position, then move your hands down to your sides. Keep your head up, but drop your gaze to the floor.

3 Slowly walk from one end of your space to the other. Then, pause, turn around and walk back. Do this several times, gradually slowing your pace as you do so and allowing yourself to be more aware of your body. Pause at each end before continuing to walk.

4 Once you have settled into the meditation, you can bring your focus to the lower legs and feet. Notice how they

feel as you move first one and then the other. It may help you to pay attention if you make a mental note of your steps – using the label 'stepping, stepping'.

5 You can continue simply marking each step as you walk back and forth, or you can slow your pace right down and can pay more detailed attention to the process of stepping.
• Notice your weight shift onto the standing foot as you raise the stepping foot into the air.
• Be aware of the motion of the raised leg as it moves forward, and the corresponding bend of the standing foot behind.
• Feel the raised heel strike the ground and then the rest of the foot rolling down.
• Notice the back heel rise off the ground behind as the front foot rolls down, when you prepare to take the next step.

6 If you are walking very slowly, you can use more detailed labels to describe the

process of your movements – 'lifting', 'moving', 'placing' are often used.

7 Just as with sitting meditation, you may find that your attention is distracted from your focus by your thoughts, feelings or sensations of the body. This is quite natural, so try to avoid berating yourself or drawing conclusions about your ability to meditate from this. Simply, gently, calmly direct your mind back to the movement of the feet.

8 At the end of your walking meditation, come to the end of your walking area and take a few mindful breaths before getting on with your day.

Walking meditation can be a good way to focus the mind, especially if you are prone to feeling sleepy during sitting meditation …

MINDFUL MOVEMENT

You can bring mindfulness to any form of physical movement. Yoga, tai chi and chi gung are all forms of mindful movement, and mindful movement is an integral part of many mindfulness courses.

Here are two simple yoga poses that you can practise as mindful movements. In some forms of yoga the emphasis is on making perfectly choreographed shapes with the body – but this is not the mindful approach. Instead, we are interested in making slow focused movements into the pose and out of the pose.

Try to keep your awareness on each movement – notice if there is a corresponding movement elsewhere in the body. Sometimes the whole body gets involved in a movement, and we make unnecessary movements out of habit, which create tension in the body. Keep the rest of the body soft when you move. Enjoy natural breathing as you move – there is no need to try to coordinate the breath and the movement.

RAISED ARMS POSE
Simple standing postures engage the whole body, and this one is a lovely stretch to do in the morning. It starts from a basic standing position (see page 80–1).

1 Stand with your feet a little distance apart and your arms by your sides. Let yourself breathe naturally, and bring your attention to the feet. Spend a little time shifting your weight from one foot to another, before coming to a position where it feels evenly balanced.

2 Move slowly from the insides to the outsides of your feet, until you feel you are in a midway position, and then shift your

weight slightly from the balls to the heels, until again you feel you are in a midway position of balance.

3 Bring your arms outward and upward in a smooth arc to meet above the head, with your palms together (go only as far as feels comfortable). Gently look up towards the hands. If you find this easy, let your gaze travel back as you drop the head backwards.

4 Slowly come out of the pose in the same gentle way, retracing your movements. Do this a few times.

FOLD FORWARDS

This yoga pose – often called the roll down – is a great way to relax the body and stretch the spine. Folding forwards and down helps to bring your attention inwards and quieten the mind. Some of us will be able to reach the toes, others will hardly fold at all. Remember that we are not interested in a goal here; we are interested in noticing what happens to the body.

1 Stand with your feet a short distance apart and let your arms hang down by your sides. Take a couple of mindful breaths as you relax into standing.

2 Slowly and attentively, drop the head forwards, bringing the chin to the chest.

3 Continue folding forward from the top of your spine downwards. Be aware that as you fold, your shoulders move forwards and downwards, and your pelvis moves backwards – the whole body is involved in this movement. Keep your head down.

4 Go as far as feels comfortable (which may not be far at all) and then pause for a few moments, noticing your breath as it moves in and out of the body.

5 Slowly and carefully come out of the fold, unrolling from the base of the spine upwards, in the reverse of how you came down. Lift the head and take a couple more breaths. You can do the roll-down a few times, but pay as much attention to the final movement as you did to the first.

OPENING *the heart*

LOVING-KINDNESS

Contemporary mindfulness teaching tends to treat the process of compassion as an integral part of the practice, but it was traditionally taught as a separate technique called loving-kindness.

Mindfulness without compassion can be clinical and unflinching. The concept of loving-kindness is a process that brings a softness and gentleness to our practice. It provides a supportive way of embracing our failings and our difficulties. In the long run, this can encourage us to observe them with far greater honesty than if our gaze was always and only uncompromising.

You could say that loving-kindness is to the heart what mindfulness is to the head. Just as we need to develop our

> *Loving-kindness is what brings a softness and gentleness to our practice. It provides a supportive way of embracing our failings and our difficulties.*

awareness and understanding – which is mindfulness – so too we need to work on our ability to be emotionally open and connected to others – which is loving-kindness.

THE LOVING-KINDNESS MEDITATION
This meditation is intended to engender goodwill towards others. One experiment by Stanford University found that practising this meditation for just a few minutes helped participants to feel more positive and more connected to strangers. Feeling connected is a basic human need, and there is plenty of research to show that our human connections bring with them health and wellbeing benefits.

More about loving-kindness
Some people find the idea and practise of loving-kindness meditation difficult – it can feel false or awkward; you may not feel anything despite your best intentions; or you may find that it makes you feel highly emotional or angry. It can take time for positive feelings to unfold, so try to be patient, and accept any objections and difficulties as part of the process. It's fine to skip parts that you find particularly hard.

1 Take a comfortable position, and close your eyes. Spend a few moments concentrating on the breath to help yourself settle into the meditation.

2 When you feel ready, bring to mind an image of yourself – either as you are now, or – if you find it easier – when you were a child. Gently say the following words to yourself:

May I be happy
May I be well
May I be safe
May I be at ease

to have a debate with yourself, but can simply note any sense of objection and continue wishing yourself well with as much gentleness and kindness as you can manage.

4 Now bring someone you love to mind: your favourite aunt, your best friend, your partner or even your dog. It should be someone that you have positive feelings about – if you are in conflict with your mother at the moment, say, then choose someone else towards whom you can feel wholeheartedly affectionate. Bring an image of this person to mind, and think of the wonderful qualities that he or she possesses. Acknowledge the fact this person – like you – is vulnerable to sickness and pain. Repeat these words as if speaking directly to him or her, repeating them over and over:
May you be happy
May you be well
May you be safe
May you be at ease

3 Keep repeating these words to yourself, with feeling, over and over again, allowing their message to permeate your mind and body. Sometimes this exercise can bring up interesting objections – perhaps you baulk at the idea of wishing yourself to be safe, as if being safe is rather boring. Or perhaps you feel you do not deserve to be happy for some reason. You do not need

5 Now extend these warm wishes to someone that you know but feel neutral about – so you neither feel liking nor disliking for him or her. This could be the person you buy a newspaper or daily coffee from, the postman or postwoman, or perhaps someone you see on the daily commute. Bring this person to mind, and acknowledge that he or she is as vulnerable to sickness and pain as you, or the people you love. Silently direct these words to him or her, repeating them several times:

May you be happy

May you be well

May you be safe

May you be at ease

6 Now think of a person that you have a difficult relationship with. You don't need to choose someone who has caused you terrible pain – that may be too great a task – but someone who you dislike or think badly of. Bring an image of the person to your mind, and acknowledge to yourself that this person wants to be happy and safe, just as we all do. Wish them well, gently repeating the phrases:

May you be happy

May you be well

May you be safe

May you be at ease

7 When you feel ready, try to imagine that the four of you are together: yourself, your loved one, your neutral person and your difficult person. Send your loving wishes to all four of you:

May we be happy

May we be well

May we be safe

May we be at ease

8 Finally, extend these feelings of compassion out further – to all those in your street, your community, your city, your country, and to all living beings in the world.

May we be happy

May we be well

May we be safe

May we be at ease

9 Slowly come out of the meditation, and open your eyes. You may like to remain seated for a couple of minutes before getting up slowly.

In your own words

You don't have to use the exact words on this page – feel free to adapt them to words that resonate more deeply with you, or that you feel more comfortable with.

KINDNESS TO YOURSELF

Many of us are far harder on ourselves than we would be to others. We need to be self-kind – and not just for our own benefit. When we look after our own needs, we are more able to extend warmth and kindness to others.

When we start to practise mindfulness, all sorts of new self-criticisms may be triggered. 'What's wrong with me?' 'I am so useless', 'I can't even sit still right' – these are all common reactions. An attitude of compassion will help us meet these thoughts with gentleness. If the idea of being kind to yourself sounds indulgent, take time to think about why. Does it feel weak to be in need of kindness? Do you feel you are in some way undeserving? Is this feeling part of a general irritation and impatience with yourself? Such queries are worth exploring.

When we start to practise mindfulness, all sorts of new self-criticisms may be triggered. 'What's wrong with me?' 'I am so useless', 'I can't even sit still right' – these are all common reactions.

PRACTISING SELF-KINDNESS
Here are some ways of increasing kindness to yourself.

Avoid harsh judgements When you notice that you are scolding or berating yourself, ask whether you would speak in this way to a friend or a relative, or a child. This can help to bring your attention back to the moment. Remind yourself that the thought is just a thought, it isn't necessarily the truth. Use kind words to describe yourself. Try to cultivate a non-critical inner voice.

Don't judge the judging Getting frustrated with yourself for being self-critical is just another trick of the unaware mind. Bring the same level of noticing to this: say 'this is judging'. And remind yourself that the judgement is just another fleeting thought.

Make time When we are busy, we tend to stop doing the things that make us happy – exercise, meditation, meeting friends. Make pleasurable activities part of your to-do list.

Acknowledge the good Notice when you do something well – cooking dinner, meeting a deadline – and make it a cause of congratulation. Say 'well done' to yourself and mean it.

Stop the shoulds How often do you do something because you feel you should? We all have duties, of course, but often we force ourselves to do all sorts of things out of guilt or a sense of obligation. If you notice yourself thinking you 'must' or 'should' do something, take a moment to examine why. Perhaps, this time, you can give yourself the gift of not doing that irksome task.

Listen to your body As you practise mindfulness you become more aware of how the body feels. Use this awareness. If you feel tired, take steps to remedy it – have an early night. Treat the ache in your wrists as you type as a sign that you need a short break. Give yourself the basics – eat when you are hungry, drink when you are thirsty, sleep when you are tired.

KINDNESS TO OTHERS

Making a conscious decision to be kind to those around you can be a life-changing element of your practice. Being kind to others can strengthen your social network, and improve many aspects of your relationships.

When we are fully aware, we are naturally more alert to the struggles of others, and may be prompted to respond with greater compassion. Research suggests that practising mindfulness, especially with the integral element of loving-kindness, can increase empathy towards others, as well as improving one's capacity for self-kindness. This is the mindfulness of human interaction, and is a central plank of the mindful approach.

In short, it is possible to nurture within oneself a habit of compassion. Here are some ways to nurture kindness to others.

DO A DAILY ACT OF KINDNESS

Give up your seat on public transport, pay for someone's coffee, allow someone to go ahead of you in the supermarket queue… Psychological studies have found that being kind to others give us a happiness boost partly because they boost levels of the happiness hormone oxytocin in the body. Researchers at the University of Columbia asked people with anxiety to do at least six acts of kindness a week – and concluded that doing nice things for others had a significant effect on the giver's mood. Even better, doing small (or large) favours for others can have a domino effect. That is to say: being on the receiving end of a kind act has been shown to make the recipient more likely to do favours for someone else further down the line. So being kind – in some small way – helps to make the world a better place.

ACKNOWLEDGE OTHERS

As we rush about our business, it is easy to forget the fact that we are dealing with other human beings who experience emotions and difficulties, just as we do. Making a conscious decision to treat

others with respect is a simple foundation of kindness. So be sure to make eye contact with all the people you come into contact with – the ticketseller at the station, the server in the sandwich shop, the person who holds a door open for you as you arrive at work.

SUPPORT YOUR LOVED ONES

Kindness has been shown to be a key factor in sustaining long-term relationships. And one of the simplest ways to be kind to others is simply to give them your attention. The spiritual teacher Thich Nhat Hanh teaches a meditation that he calls 'Darling I am here for you'. All it involves is setting aside distractions so that you can truly engage with a loved one.

LET IT GO

As well as seeking to be actively kind we can also strengthen our capacity for letting go. If you find the trivial misdemeanour of others easily irritate you, then try making a point of not reacting at least once a day. Rather than showing your disapproval in deeds or words, notice your thoughts and feelings and let them go.

MINDFUL INTERACTIONS

Bringing mindfulness to your relationships doesn't have to be a complex process. Simply being truly present can make a difference to the way you are around those closest to you.

When we are in conversation with someone we know well, we often make a show of listening when in reality we are merely pretending. Mindful listening involves focusing on what the other person is expressing in their words, facial expressions and body language. So if, for example, you notice yourself rehearsing your next contribution, silently acknowledge that and bring your attention back to the other person.

When someone is speaking to you, be receptive without interrupting, judging or discounting what is said. You don't have to agree with the person – you are simply allowing them to express what they want without interruption. This is a fundamental of good communication.

Mindful listening involves focusing on what the other person is expressing in their words, facial expressions and body language.

Of course, you may have an emotional or physical response as you listen – upset, tension in the belly, a clenching of the jaw. You can be aware of these sensations without allowing them to dictate your responses. Arguments often follow familiar paths: if you do not rise to the bait, then the conversation may be more positive.

As you practise mindful listening, you will become more adept at noticing the mental habits you have in conversation. Perhaps you are quick to jump in with advice, or divert the conversation to a story of your own. It takes time to change unhelpful tendencies but awareness is always a good first step.

Speaking mindfully is just as important as listening. If you can bring awareness to what you say, you can prevent much strife.

• **Pause before you answer** This allows you to think about the content and tone of what you want to say. Bringing space into an exchange can prevent hasty words.

• **Speak truthfully** This doesn't mean you need to share everything, but what you do say should be authentic and reflect the reality of your experience. Watch the tendency to exaggerate – 'You always do this', 'I never get a chance to do that'.

• **Speak kindly** Mindful speech means not using words to create discord. Avoid comments that wound or raise the stakes. Watch how you speak about yourself – self-deprecation or self-criticism can be as damaging as speaking harshly to others.

• **Speak calmly** There are times when you feel emotional and need to express yourself of course, but in ordinary conversation it is best to keep your tone civil and calm.

• **Avoid gossip** This is a hard one for many of us. But mindfulness of speech means not engaging in idle chatter about other people.

GRATITUDE

A sense of appreciation often flourishes when we practise mindfulness. As we become more conscious of the realities of our day-to-day life, we are more able to notice and appreciate what we have.

It would be a mistake to think that mindfulness teaches that everything is wonderful – it doesn't. The core insight of mindfulness is that we all too easily think in ways that are bound to make us unhappy. When we live in a cloud of regret about the past or of anxiety about the future, we miss out on so many of the simple gifts and pleasures that life has to offer us *right now*: the smile of a child, a great cup of coffee, the company of a friend or the familiar comfort of our own front room.

In general, moments of pleasure and relief are available to us during even the most difficult day. We can always take a second to appreciate how our morning toast tastes, or to acknowledge the efficient help of a shop assistant. Making a point of noticing these moments can help us to feel more positive about our lives, and it can have an effect on our health too. In one well-known experiment by psychologist Robert A Emmons, three groups of participants were asked to write either about things they were grateful for each day, or about things that irritated them, or else about neutral events. At the end of the study, the 'grateful' group felt happier and more optimistic than the neutral or negative group.

In general, moments of pleasure and relief are available to us during even the most difficult day.

Further experiments by Emmons and others have shown that practising gratitude can improve levels of happiness, which in turn can boost physical and mental wellbeing. Try these ways to sharpen your sense of gratitude:

1 As in Emmons's experiment, spend a few minutes a day writing down five things that you are thankful for. The very act of writing helps these things to stick in your mind, and also you'll be more aware of the blessings in your life. Before you start writing, take a few mindful breaths to bring yourself into the moment – and enjoy recalling your occasions for gratitude. Or try writing your journal once a week – one experiment showed that weekly journalling had greater benefits than doing it daily, perhaps because people were less likely to see it as a chore.

2 Express thanks. As you go about your day, seek out reasons for expressions of gratitude – say thank you to the driver as

you get off the bus, the colleague who volunteers to make the teas, the postman who delivers a parcel. And try to say thank you like you mean it – make eye contact and smile, or tell them how much you have appreciated what they have done.

3 Write a letter. These days we are more likely to send an email or an online message than a physical note. But writing a letter of thanks can be a tremendously worthwhile exercise for you, and a real gift to the recipient. Think of someone who has done a lot for you – a parent, a good friend, a mentor or teacher. Put in words what he or she has done, and what it has meant to you.

Quick blessing count

Counting your blessings can be a great way to come into the moment. Pause, and count five things on your fingers that you are thankful for right now: your health, your new shoes, a problem solved or a crisis averted…

DIFFICULT EMOTIONS

Turbulent emotions are a part of life. We all get angry, sad or overwhelmed from time to time but these emotions are temporary, they no more represent the truth of our emotional life than one wet spell defines a summer.

One effect of a regular meditation practice is that our emotions gradually become more regulated, less prone to wild fluctuations. So over time we tend to feel more in control. By understanding that we are not our feelings, we can maintain a little space between them and ourselves. When it comes to tricky emotions, mindfulness reminds us to 'be' rather than 'do'. If we can learn to 'be' with painful feelings rather than distracting ourselves from them or expressing them in unhealthy ways, then we can prevent them from pushing us towards unhelpful actions.

> *By understanding that we are not our feelings, we can maintain a little space between them and ourselves.*

But painful emotions can still seem so strong that they threaten to overwhelm us, like a breaking wave. Here is a mindfulness technique that can be useful in these moments; its four stages spell out the acronym RAIN.

THE RAIN TECHNIQUE

R: Recognising Sometimes intense emotions catch us unawares – we may not realise that we are angry until we find ourselves snapping, for example. So, noticing that the presence of a strong emotion is the first stage in the RAIN technique. Being aware that an emotion is there and pausing to give it a label – anger, sadness, loneliness, jealousy – can be helpful. If an uncomfortable emotion is difficult to label it is fine to call it 'discomfort' or some other general term.

A: Accepting You can't make an unpleasant emotion disappear simply by wishing it away or ignoring it. Acceptance is a key part of mindfulness, and is one of the most useful tools for dealing with emotion. Make space for the emotion that is there. Say to yourself 'I am feeling anger' or 'anger is present'.

I: Investigating Bring the mindful attitude of curiosity to this emotion – how does it feel in the body, where is it present, is it moving? What thoughts are you aware of? Can you sit and simply examine this emotion in real time?

N: Non-identifying As you investigate your emotion, you can develop a sense of distance from it – a recognition that you are not your emotion. That recognition is what the term 'non-identifying' means. Your current emotion – like all emotions – is a temporary state of the body and the mind, and – like all states of mind and body – will arise, be present and then pass in time. This may happen while you sit and breathe, or it may take longer. Be patient.

RAIN for addiction

Addictive behaviours can also be helped by the RAIN approach. If you are trying to give up smoking, for example, then you can use the RAIN technique to sit with and work through the urge for a cigarette.

EMBRACE FORGIVENESS

We can make the mistake of reigniting old feelings of pain or anger through our thoughts. Holding a grudge, for example, is sometimes nothing other than clinging to negative emotions that we should try to let go.

Learning to forgive can release us from old patterns of thought and old emotional injuries, and so make us happier in the end. Forgiveness is making a conscious effort to release angry or vengeful thoughts towards a person that you feel has harmed you. That doesn't mean forgetting what has happened or even maintaining a relationship with the person – because it may well be sensible to protect yourself from someone who has harmed you in the past. Forgiveness means letting go of the pain of the past, and opening up to the possibilities of the present. This exercise can be helpful if you want to work on forgiveness, but it is important to approach it with compassion for yourself. You cannot force forgiveness or decide that the will is there when it isn't. You just have to make space for it to appear.

1 Take a comfortable position, close your eyes and breathe for a few moments. When you feel ready, think of the person who has caused you harm. Remember to bring an attitude of compassion towards yourself – don't push yourself to remember details that you find painful.

2 As you reflect on this person, be aware of what is happening in your body. When we bring to mind a difficult event from the past we often relive it in some sense – our body may become tense, there may be tightness in the throat, and we may experience emotions of sadness. Notice these feelings, and give them a label if you can – 'tightness', 'grief' and so on.

3 Reflect on the fact that you are experiencing these painful feelings, not the person or people that caused you the pain. So you are suffering in this way, but they are not (though of course they may have their own difficulties to contend with).

4 Now try to clarify what is preventing you from letting go of the anger you feel, or stopping you from forgiving this person or group. Are you afraid that forgiving will make you vulnerable in some way? Do you feel someone else will 'win' if you let go of your anger?

5 Consider the other person. Do you think he or she might see what happened differently? Or think about the type of

person he or she is, and perhaps what you know about his or her home life or background? Is there anything that might explain the event, or allow you to see him or her as a person in need of compassion?

6 If this is too difficult, no matter. Remember you cannot force yourself into an attitude of forgiveness, so these ideas are simply suggestions to help you find a starting point to work with. The point is to explore ways of making space for forgiveness by letting go of old pain and emotional blockages. Allow the process to unfold naturally.

7 Check in with yourself and with the breath as you reflect – are you breathing naturally or has the breath changed? Is there greater tension in the body or less – or have your feelings and emotions changed in some way? You can return to this exercise at any point. For now, spend a few moments breathing before opening your eyes slowly.

LIVING WITH PAIN

Mindfulness is increasingly being used as a way of helping people to manage chronic pain. Most of us have to deal with physical discomfort in our lives, and for some people pain is a part of daily life.

Pain is more than just an alarm signal from the body. Our understanding of how the pain mechanism works is incomplete, but one theory is that there are pain 'gates' to the brain and nervous system, and that pain signals can only pass through when the gates are opened. We also know that the brain uses information from the mind (our thoughts and feelings) as well as the body to make sense of pain – so it is a psychological and emotional phenomenon as well as a physical one.

It follows that we may be able to use our minds to change our perception of pain – and this is where mindfulness comes in. Mindfulness can also help in another way. If we consider the 'two arrows' story again, we are reminded that there are two types of pain – the raw physical data (the first arrow, or primary pain), and the mental anguish that surrounds it (the second arrow, or secondary pain). If we can learn to distinguish between these two types of pain, we can help to relieve ourselves of

some of the suffering that we feel from the second arrow.

Mindfulness encourages us to notice and acknowledge our pain. Of course we want to be rid of it – but pain can sometimes be a burden that we have to carry. If we cannot be rid of it, then we

Mindfulness teaches us to move towards pain and explore it with an attitude of acceptance and compassion.

often move into judgements – 'I hate this pain', 'Why is this happening to me', 'I can't bear this'. Such reactions heighten our distress and can exacerbate the pain. It's a vicious cycle: the more we fret about our pain, the greater the pain can feel; the more intense the pain, the more we worry.

We often think of pain as a single sensation of 'pain', but if we can investigate it with an attitude of gentle interest we discover that there is no single unchanging body of pain that we feel. Instead our pain is made up of lots of different sensations. These may become intense and then fade away, they may be intermittent rather than constant, moving rather than static – as we explore our pain we discover that there are gaps in the pain or times when it lessens.

Mindfulness teaches us to move towards pain and explore it with an attitude of acceptance and compassion. This may sound counterintuitive, but brain imaging has shown that it can reduce the distress we feel about it. Practising the body scan (page 96–8) can be helpful, or you can try this exercise to explore pain.

THE PAIN MEDITATION

1 Sit or lie down as comfortably as you can, and close your eyes and mouth. Breathe naturally for a few moments, paying attention to the passage of air into the nostrils, and then out again.

2 As you breathe in, imagine that the breath is travelling from the nostrils to the area where the pain is.

3 As you breathe out imagine that the breath begins in the painful area and then makes its way out of the body. When we are in pain, our muscles tense up, which can make the pain feel worse. Breathing this way encourages the muscles to relax.

4 Notice any thoughts or emotions that come back – there may be a sense of fear or panic, sadness or anger. Perhaps you will notice the thoughts 'this is never going to end' or 'I can't bear this' or 'I am so unlucky'. These are just thoughts that you can notice and allow to pass. It is natural to judge and push away our pain but by allowing it to be, by softening and making space for it, we can become more accepting of our current reality.

5 Allow your attention to settle on your pain as you breathe naturally. As best you can, explore the reality of your pain. This can be very challenging; be kind to yourself and do what you can. If it starts to feel overwhelming, go back to the breath until you feel ready to try again.

6 Notice if expectations come up as you are doing this exercise – remember that mindfulness is about being with what is rather than actively trying to change it. So don't worry if your pain does not lessen or if you find the exercise difficult. Just keep exploring and registering the pain with an attitude of curiosity and acceptance.

7 If you feel an urge to change position, notice the urge, and then go ahead and change position. But try to avoid fidgeting and constant movement.

8 Remember that all you need to do is to be with the pain in this moment – you do not have to think about the next minutes or hours, or days ahead. Stay in the reality of the present.

9 When you are ready to end the meditation, bring your attention back to the breath for a few moments, then open your eyes slowly.

INDEX

This edition is published by Lorenz Books, an imprint of Anness Publishing Ltd
www.lorenzbooks.com; www.annesspublishing.com
info@anness.com

Anness Publishing has a new picture agency outlet for images for publishing,
promotions or advertising. Please visit our website www.practicalpictures.com
for more information.

A CIP catalogue record for this book is available from the British Library.

Publisher: Joanna Lorenz
Senior Editor: Joanne Rippin
Designer: Nigel Partridge
Production: Ben Worley

PUBLISHER'S NOTE
The reader should not regard the recommendations, ideas and techniques expressed
and described in this book as substitutes for the advice of a qualified medical
practitioner or other qualified professional. Any use to which the recommendations,
ideas and techniques are put is at the reader's sole discretion and risk.

KIM DAVIES
Kim Davies is an established writer in the field of natural health and
well-being. She is the author of more than 20 books, including titles on
yoga, tai chi and happiness. She first came across mindfulness while
studying meditation in India in 2000, and has practised it ever since. She
regularly writes on mindfulness for books and magazines.